COMMERCIAL DIRECTING
VOODOO

Filmmaking Spells
& Production Potions

WRITTEN & ILLUSTRATED BY JORDAN BRADY

"This is the bible for commercial directing. Read it, learn it, live by it. It's all the stuff veteran directors wish they had been told at the beginning of their careers."

-- Chuck Meehan, EVP/ECD Doner

ISBN-13: 978-1986181020

ISBN-10: 1986181022

Written and poorly illustrated by Jordan Brady, all rights reserved. No portion of this book can be reprinted or used without prior written consent from the author. Be cool and please do not steal this book, literally or electronically.

©Brady Oil Entertainment 2018

My websites:

www.jordanbrady.com

www.commercialdirectingbootcamp.com

www.iambattlecomic.com

www.iamroadcomic.com

www.osodelicious.org

www.superlounge.tv

ACKNOWLEDGEMENTS

Most of all, hugest thank you to Jeannette Godoy, my fabulous wife, lover and partner. To my amazing kids Jake, Ben, Gabi and Gigi. Y'all are my chief motivators in this life.

Thanks mom. You have encouraged and supported every creative endeavor that I've had. My lil' sister Muriel too!

I'm very grateful to the talented filmmakers: the artists, technicians, crew, directors, producers, writers, editors, vfx wizards, sales reps, composers, mixers and executive producers and everyone that has taught me their tricks.

Shout out to each and every guest that's appeared on my popular podcast, Respect The Process. Your candid interviews have taught me so much about craft and myself. Collectively we have paid it forward by sharing our experiences.

Of course, thanks to each and every advertising agency creative. Those copywriters, art directors and creative directors that created the ideas and then foolishly trust me to shepherd their scripts to life. It all starts with a great idea.

Most of all, kudos to clients that take chances with their ads.

FORWARD

I first met Jordan Brady in the Summer of '98, (not sure it was actually the Summer, but it makes for a better first line). I was a young copywriter on my way up and he was just starting his directing career. I just sold a funny concept for a car brand and was looking for a director who could bring the funny. We didn't have a lot of time or a lot of budget, so I'd like to say we picked Jordan due to his extensive reel and experience. But as he really hadn't done an actual commercial yet, just some comedy shorts and a few promos, we picked him because he and his company could do it for the money. That leap of faith, on both our parts, has led to a 20 year relationship of creating all kinds of hilarious, engaging stories that have helped build numerous brands. Not to mention both of our reels. And when it comes to budgets, he has a unique ability to make a penny look like a nickel.

Every time I work with Jordan I learn something new. About comedy, storytelling, timing, acting, even how to collaborate more effectively. And all that is in here. All of his experience, knowledge and talent is yours for the taking.

He's always told me that it all starts with a good script. Well if you want to be a successful director it all starts with this book.

Enjoy.

Chuck Meehan, EVP/ECD Doner

Put yourself in a box.

Artists want to a have a varied body of work. Screw that. Strive to be known for doing one specific style of filmmaking really well. I know a director that had a hit with a spot starring a chimp, so he become the go-to director for chimp work.

I'm a comedy dialogue director. Can I shoot lovely lifestyle work? You bet. But this world is about selling yourself. The sooner you define what it is that you do, the easier it is for others to sell you. So don't wait for the industry to categorize you. Put yourself in that box.

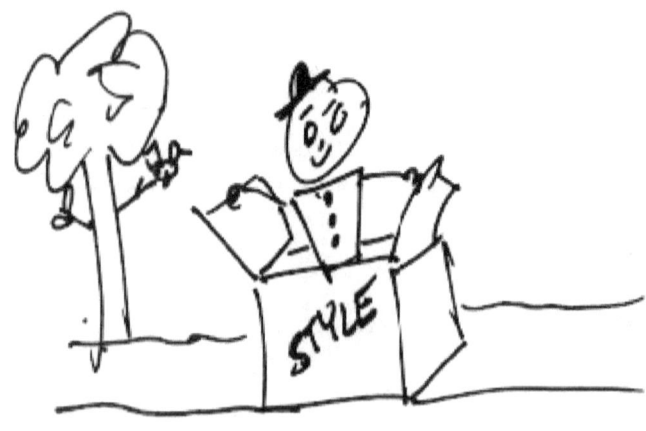

Know what you want.

If you really want to make that romantic comedy independent feature and strive to be the next Nora Ephron, then by golly you go for it. Maybe commercial directing is not the best focus of your time. It's hard to dabble in. If you look at directing spots as a hobby, you'll very likely fail.

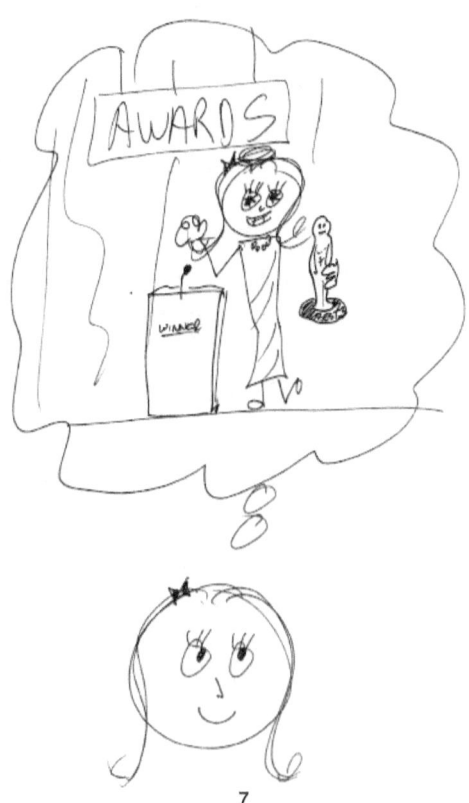

A reason to say "yes".

When I get a storyboard from an ad agency, my default reaction is to love the project. Primarily, I am always looking to add great spots to my reel. My reel is my lifeblood. But unless it's just dog shit, there is always a reason to engage and at least talk to the agency creative team. What other work have they done? Hey, I'm always looking for new relationships.

Maybe this is a chance to try a new approach to casting? Or go ahead and try working with that hot new director of photography, or use that crazy old German lens that Stanley Kubrick always used? Or simply put, it's good money.

If you listen to my podcast, Respect The Process, every decision about work is made by examining the three R's:

REEL. RELATIONSHIP. REVENUE.

Manage your career right, and it all leads to the fourth R:

REPEAT BUSINESS.

Don't expect folks to read your mind.

Filmmaking is collaborative so you need to express your thoughts and never assume people can read your mind. This is an overall approach to filmmaking. You have to express your vision to an ad agency to get work, and then to your crew so you can execute that vision if you're lucky enough to get the gig. Then in post, it helps to explain how the puzzle pieces go together.

The more specific and concise your descriptions, the more other people can help you achieve your dreams.

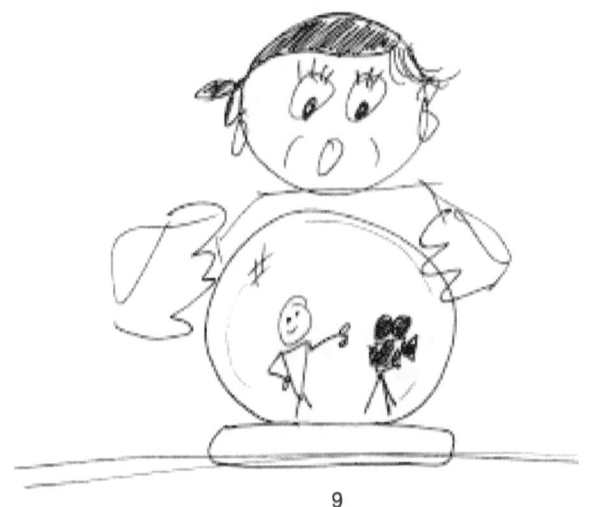

Print, scribble & draw.

It's too easy to open a script or storyboard on your phone and read it. Try this instead: Print it out, and as you read it for the very first time, scribble notes and draw images that come to mind as you go. I even try to guess the end of the spot.

Doodling as you go, on that printed page will inspire yet more ideas. What questions come to mind? Does the doctor character have to be a man? Could he be riding a pony? Let your imagination run wild.

When you do a conference call, which is essentially the job interview, you've got a plan. Maybe think twice before pitching the doctor on the pony.

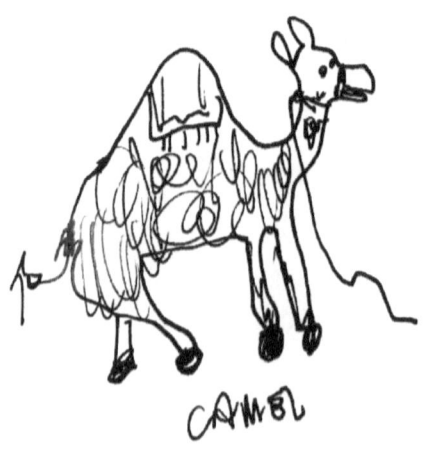

Tech Scout Preamble.

When you do the technical scout with your key crew, tell them the story you are trying to tell. Shot by shot and then some. Take them through like you'd pitch a Hollywood movie to the studio. Why? It informs these technicians of your vision so that they can rally behind your idea. Perhaps they can contribute now that they get it.

On a practical level, it saves you from answering the same questions many times over. And it can help answer logistical concerns, such as where to park equipment trucks so that they're not in the shots. It helps the 1st Assistant Director make her schedule

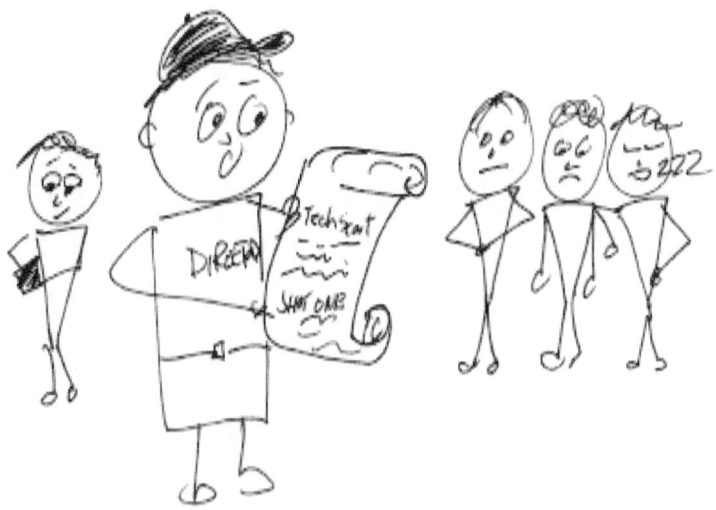

Scout for sound.

If that perfect house you've chosen is in the flight path of a major airport, you're going to regret it when recording dialogue. I will actually Google an address to see the surroundings. Is there a large industrial plant next door that will be making noise?

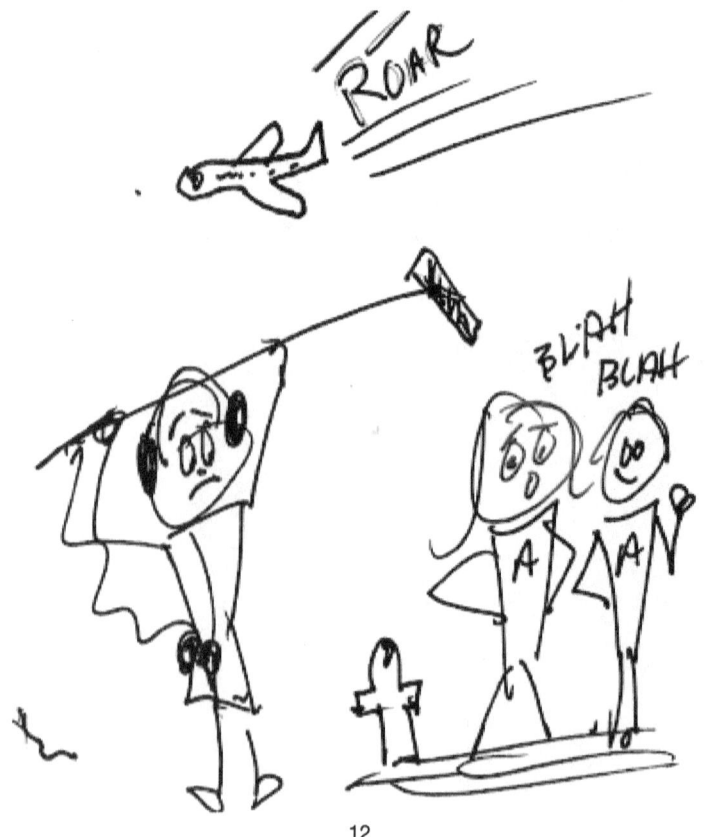

Snack while lighting.

I like to stand on set rather than sit in that director's chair. It keeps the energy up on set and there is so much to accomplish every shoot day. But you must allow the crew to do their jobs and sometimes that means stepping away from the set to give the technicians some breathing room.

I use this time to snack on healthy veggies, like carrot sticks or jicama, that round, bulbous root vegetable from the Mexican peninsula. Watermelon with spicy salt is good too.

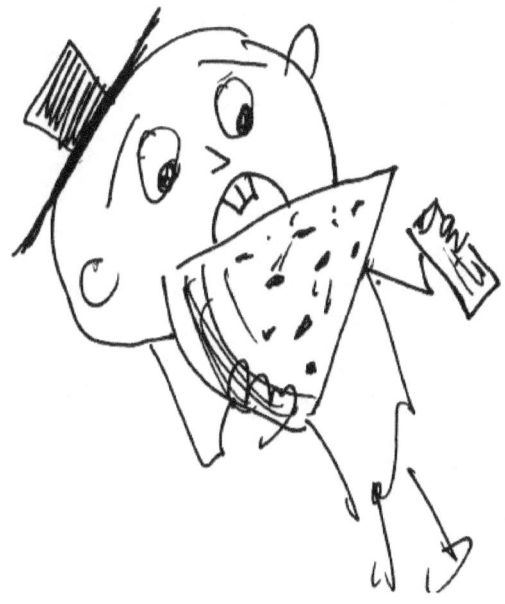

Go dark between shots.

The camera is hooked up to a live monitor so you, your client and agency friends sitting in "video village" can see what's being shot. In the old days of 35mm film cameras, a video-camera was tapped into the camera for this purpose. The live feed had to be disconnected and reconnected after each frame was set.

Nowadays, the tendency is to leave that feed up all day, so the shot is being constructed in real time before everyone's discerning eye. I hate this. It invites comments on framing, set dressing and lighting before the time to comment. An agency friend once remarked how that shot he just saw. The "shot" moving across the lawn was so cool. He thought we were practicing a dolly shot, but it was just grips moving the camera. That live feed betrayed me.

Ever since, I insist that video village feed "go dark" between camera set ups, so when we turn on the live feed, we can discuss my great frame and collaborate to make it even better.

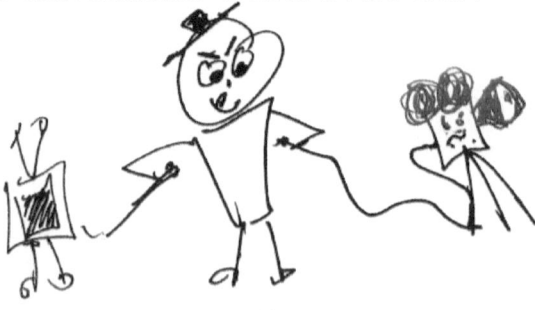

Think of your reel.

Your director's reel is your life blood. It all starts with your reel. So when you plan your shots, always think how this will live on your reel among your body of spots.

Can you shoot an extra shot?

Is there any wardrobe that will make this more special?

Is there a cinematographer who will add value to your work?

Are you settling with the casting choices?

With every opportunity that arises, you want to ask yourself: what is that extra thing I can do for my reel? What scene, reaction, line, subtle raise of an eye, that will make this an A+ spot?

If you can build it…

I am lucky to have built a twenty foot toaster prop, a two inch gasoline can and a twelve foot spatula. Sure, they could have easily been created in GC, but where's the fun in that? There's an intrinsic "joie de vivre" in making stuff.

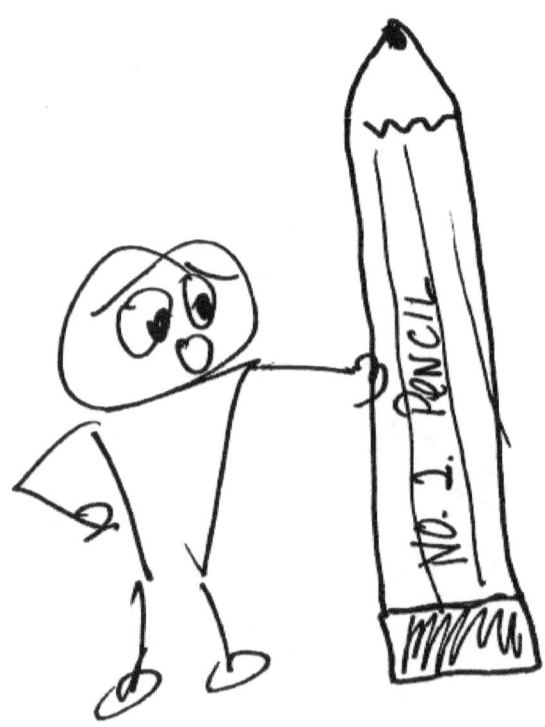

The practical effect offers an experience.

When you can pull off an effect in-camera, I swear you can feel the excitement shared by the entire cast, crew, client & agency. I'm the first to embrace digital effects and trickery, especially when it subtly enhances the work. But the more you can deliver on set, the better.

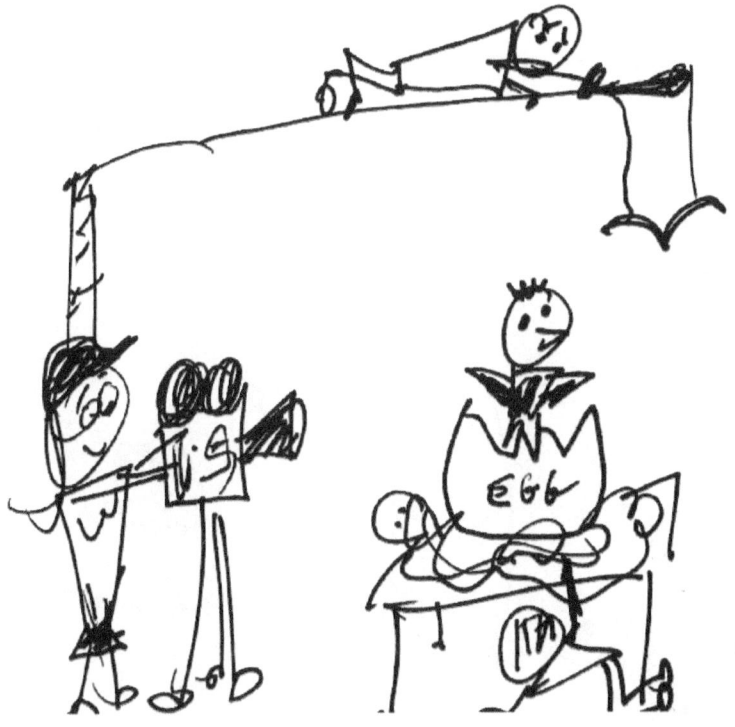

Adapt or Die.

In life, in any profession, we are often judged on how well we react to unforeseen problems. Stuff will go wrong at any stage of the filmmaking process and that is part of the rush, knowing challenges await! So as the Director, you should lead your team with the mantra "there are only solutions in filmmaking."

Or die.

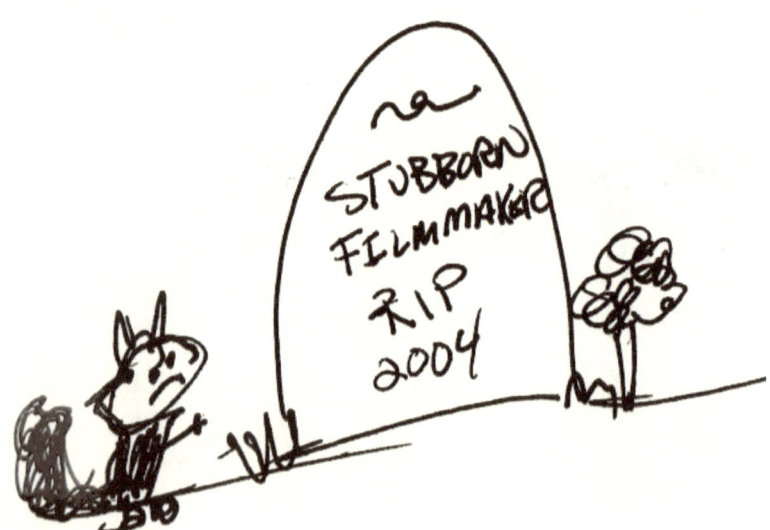

Shoot tests.

You can shoot a test of anything with your phone. Even if it is just to see how to frame two shots that may play back to back, I think it is worth getting your girlfriend and a stuffed animal to act for you.

Effects are tricky, but watch a few YouTube tutorials and you'll have the wizards at Lucas Film shaking. Okay, not really. But you can mess around and see what works. Show your crude tests to VFX experts for feedback. It's the starting point of an ongoing conversation.

One of the best uses of simple tests is so you can time out the spot and see how everything fits. I've even scanned storyboard or drawings and laid them on a time-line. It provides wonderful piece of mind.

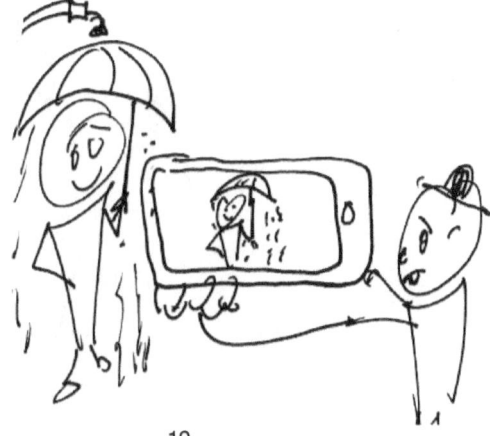

Make crew shoot tests.

Is the fake money really going to fly out of the leaf blower? Let's not wait until the shoot day and have everyone watch your prop master fiddle and discover what works. Test it.

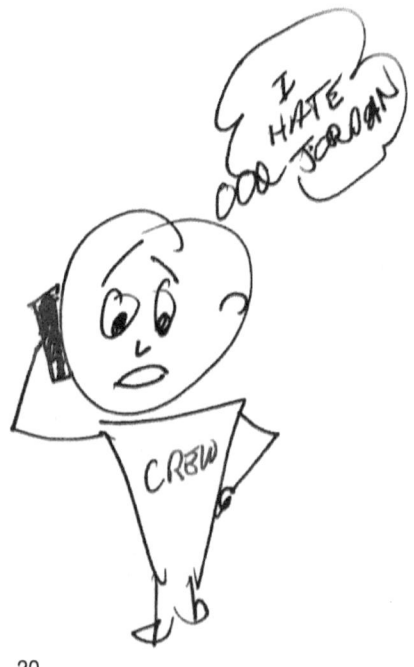

Stick People.

Invest twelve minutes and learn to draw stick people. If you can get the nose to point in the correct direction the character is looking, you're set and you can tell the story.

Moreover, the act of drawing allows the brain to think of other shots. You'll work out the shots you need. Personally, it helps me eliminate the fat out of my shot list. And if you have a great storyboard artist, your initial call will have a running start if you send them your embarrassing etchings.

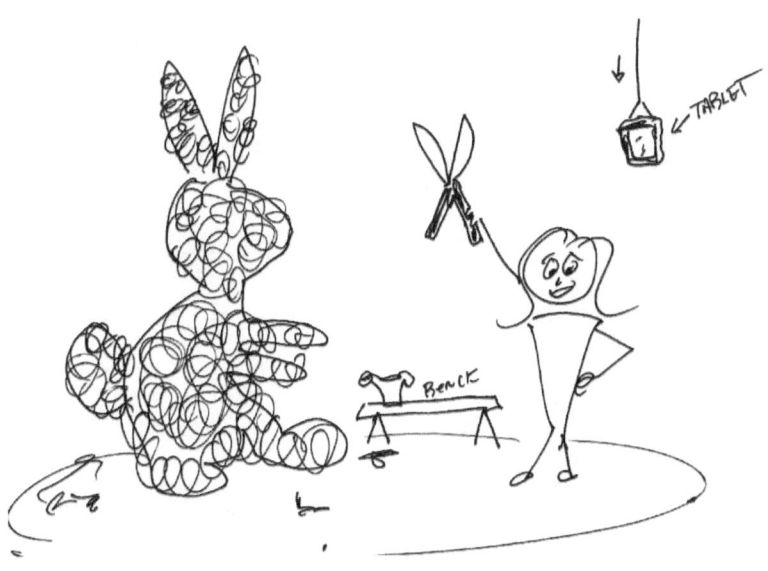

Always get those complimentary angles.

We were filming a husband and wife in the car, and falling behind schedule. We had the front two shot through the windshield, and the husband's coverage. The agency suggested we omit the coverage of the wife, citing we "had enough of her in the two shot." While dropping the wife's shots would indeed put us back on track, I refused. Can you imagine how poorly that would edit? With no coverage of the wife?

We shot a few takes and made up the time elsewhere. In the edit, it was crucial to timing for the editor to carve performance and ultimately make the spot fit the thirty seconds.

There's a little bird and her name is "Integrity". Sometimes she lands right on your shoulder and says, "deliver what's best for the commercial, not just what is required." Then that little bird takes flight and shits on your head as she flies away.

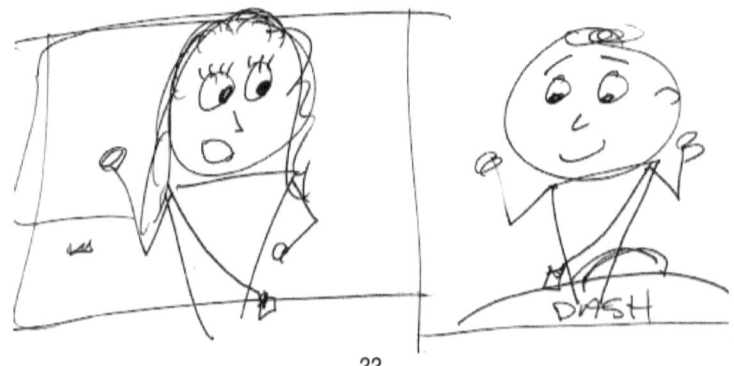

Time the spot.

Ad agencies should give stopwatches out to all the copywriters and art directors. They often seem to think that their two page script with 14 point font will make a great :15 second spot.

It is your responsibility to time out the script realistically and shoot it so the material will edit into the time allotted. There is no blaming anyone. Remember, only solutions in filmmaking. Don't pass off the problem to the editor. Know what you are doing.

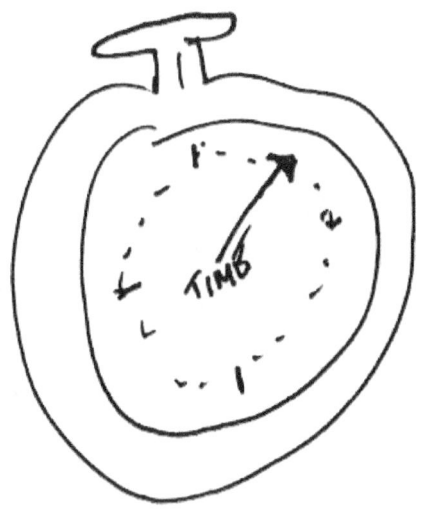

Always board less.

The old phrase "under promise, over deliver" comes to mind when drawing or planning shots. I think a :30 second spot can be told in twelve shots and often I'll trim to nine, just so it's all on one page. I don't draw every lens change either.

Of course, I've got more shots I'd love to do, but it is far better to squeeze more in a day than having to cut shots that you pitched. Basic rule is you want to under promise and over deliver.

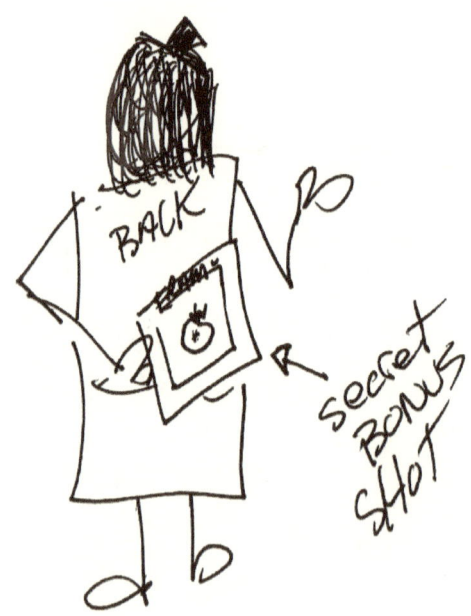

Bonus shots. Shh.

So those shots I cut, that we know will be helpful, but not crucial? Keep them in your back pocket, literally. I print those shots and show my crew, so when we can squeeze them into our shoot day, each department is prepared. If they don't know, they'll scramble and something will screw up.

You never want the bonus shot to be the "bone us" shot.

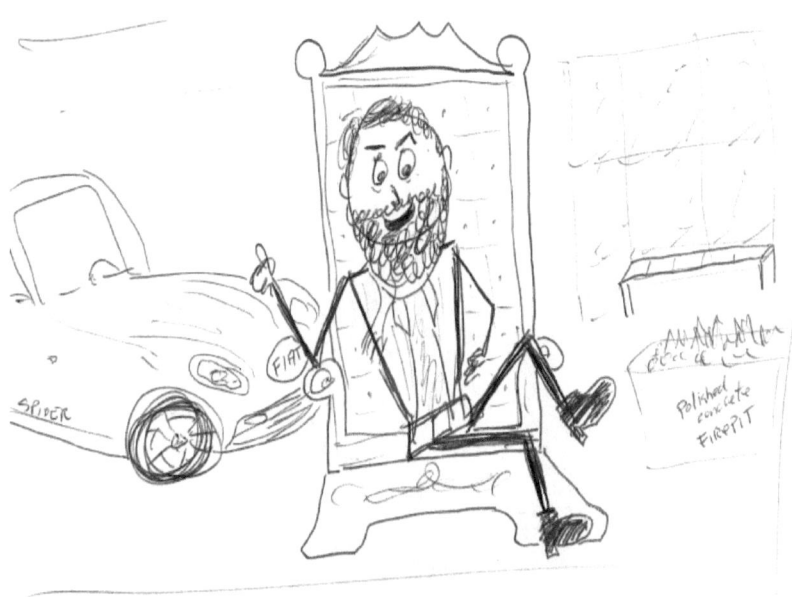

Only take shooting boards to work.

If you've done your prep, the only thing you need on the shoot day is your shot list or storyboards. And actually the 1st AD has both, but I like having my shooting boards because I've scribbled notes during the pre-production meeting on them.

The script supervisor has the script, and those words change too many times. I've killed a small rain forest just trying to print the many versions. But my shots are my bible.

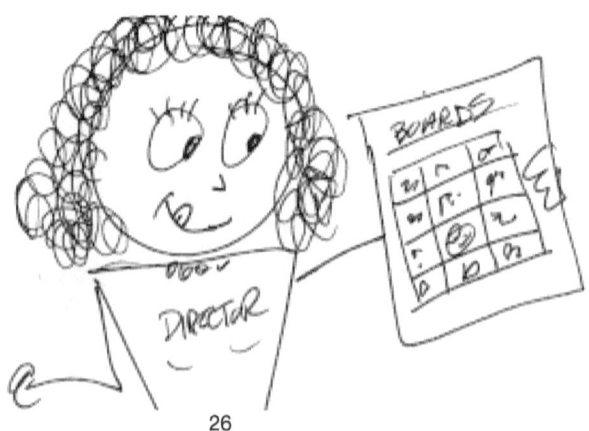

Stay downstairs.

Whenever the script calls for an upstairs bedroom, I ask myself "what does the camera see?" You can usually cheat a bedroom by bringing a bed and night tables into a living room, offering you more room for lights, camera and staging. Plus you and the agency art director can collab on the best bedroom.

Trying to cram gear plus a half dozen extra large sweaty grips and electricians into an upstairs bedroom is not always the best use of time. And on film, who knew?

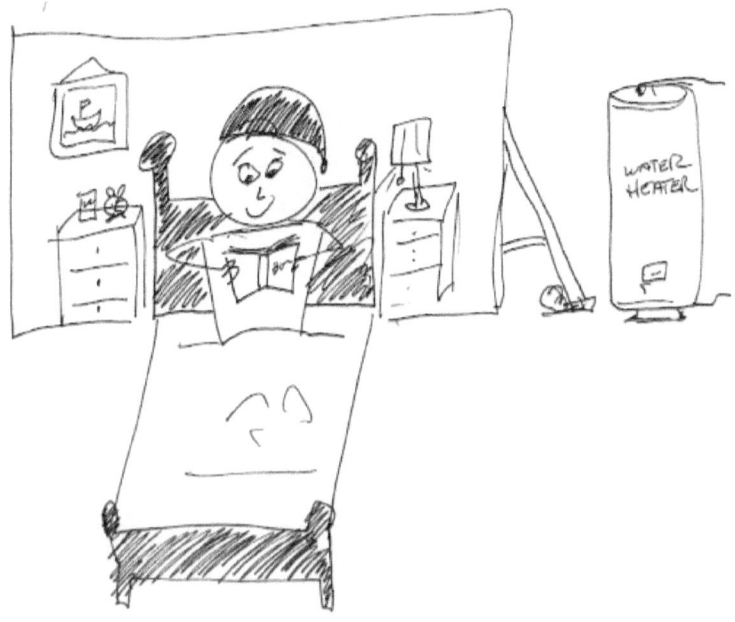

The Brady Method.

The casting director running the final audition, aka the callback session, hands you each actor's headshot. When that actor leaves the room, I decide right then if that performer is right for the part. The photo goes into one of two piles of headshots. Is that actor Dead or Alive?

At the end of the session, I lay out actors from the Alive pile onto a table and make the cast. I do that alone and offer the agency creative in the session a pee break.

Then the agency and I review the casting selections. Very rarely do we resurrect the dead. Sure the agency check notes they've scribbled and ask why so & so is dead, and I'm happy to review. But c'mon, you know as soon as you see it.

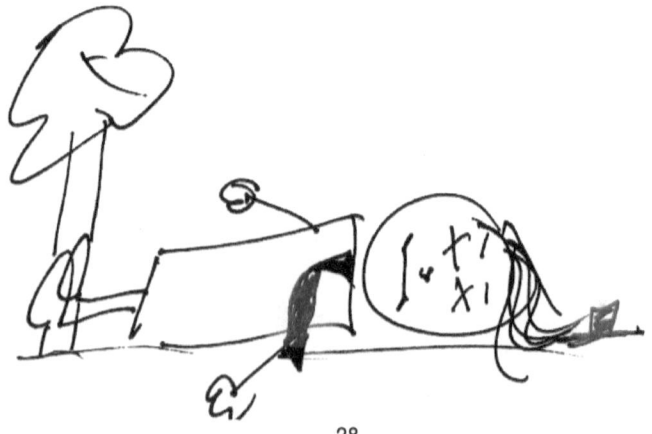

Range is overrated.

When someone says, "we'll get a range of performance" I will typically respond that we need to know going into the shoot what our preferred tone is. There's not time to explore the character in a commercial. Save that for your opus with Daniel Day Lewis.

You get the performance the actor does at the final audition. And if you do shoot a range, then the editor will choose. I prefer to choose before the shoot, not after. Obviously, sometimes you need a subtle range or alternate lines, but tonally, you want to stay in the pocket, as we say.

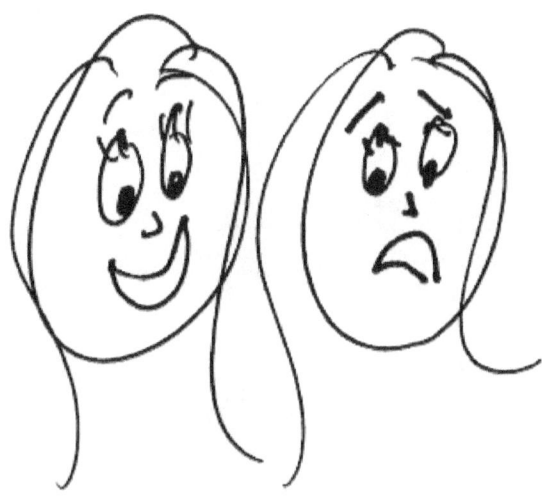

Were kid actors well-behaved?

Some Hollywood kid actors know how to audition really well. Too well. So take a peek in the hallway. Were they spoiled brats before and after coming in the room to meet you? An audition is five minutes, but you've got to shoot the entire day with them.

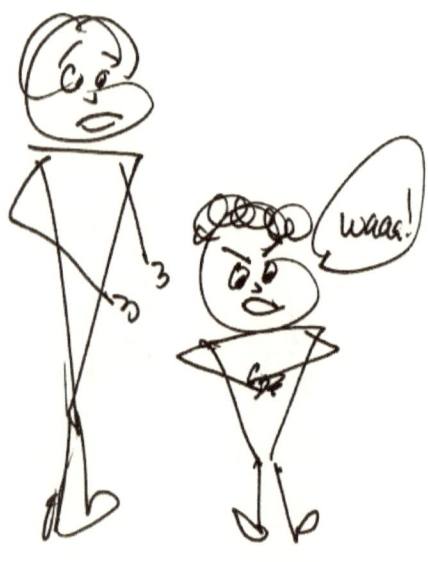

School the parents.

On a Happy Meal shoot, I just could not figure out why the young boy was listless and not responding on set with the same vigor he had at the audition. Finally his parents admitted they gave him a double dose of his medication to "help us" with his first role in a commercial. They meant well, but really boned us.

Tell the parents not to do anything different, and no big bowl of sweetened cereal in the morning. That sugar crash can be deadly on set.

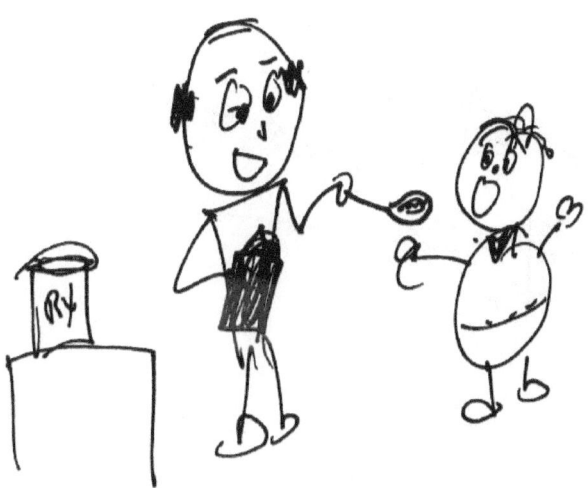

Coverage over takes.

Does it really get better after sixteen takes? No it doesn't. So after a few takes, I change the camera angle or at least the lens size so the editor can cut the scene together. Otherwise you're stuck choosing one take from a dozen, versus crafting a nice scene with a variety of angles to keep things interesting and make your reel stand out.

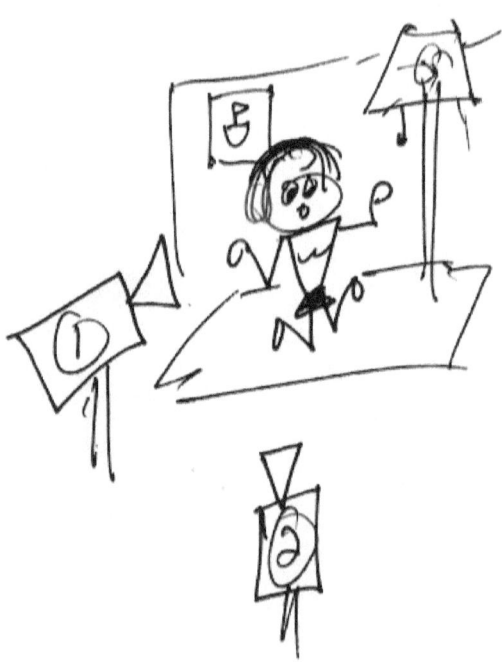

Think about the edit.

We all agreed that the spot needed to open and end on the cool car we were shooting. "The car is the star." So after we shot the dialogue in various sizes, I was surprised when this seasoned agency producer said, "we never shot the first line in a close up." "I know," I replied, "because we'll never use that shot in the edit. We open on the wide shot of the hero hot rod."

"But what if we wanted to have that option in the edit?"

"You'd screw up our great car commercial." I said respectfully.

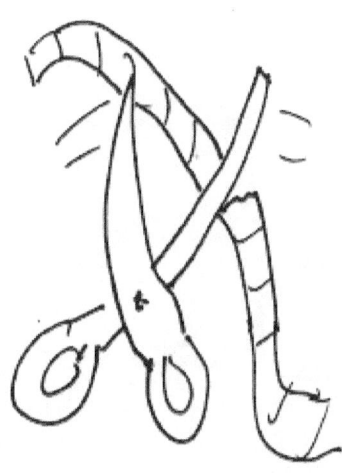

Shoot a reaction.

A reaction almost always makes any story more interesting and certainly funnier. Google "I'll have what she's having!" It is the classic reaction. Even a non-verbal reaction to someone witnessing the action can add context to a spot.

Practically speaking, a well-placed reaction shot can also allow you to bridge two takes together or get you out of a sticky continuity jam.

So, fellow filmmaker, please always try and grab that reaction shot. Could be the best seven minutes you ever spent on set.

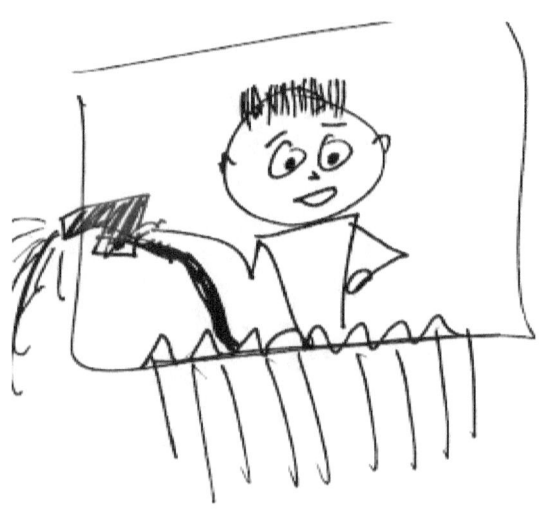

Change the lens.

I'm a huge fan of changing the lens without moving the camera, after three or for takes. This is again for editorial reasons. These days, we can blow up a 4K shot and that is handy. But capturing a different take, from a new focal length, in-camera is always way cooler.

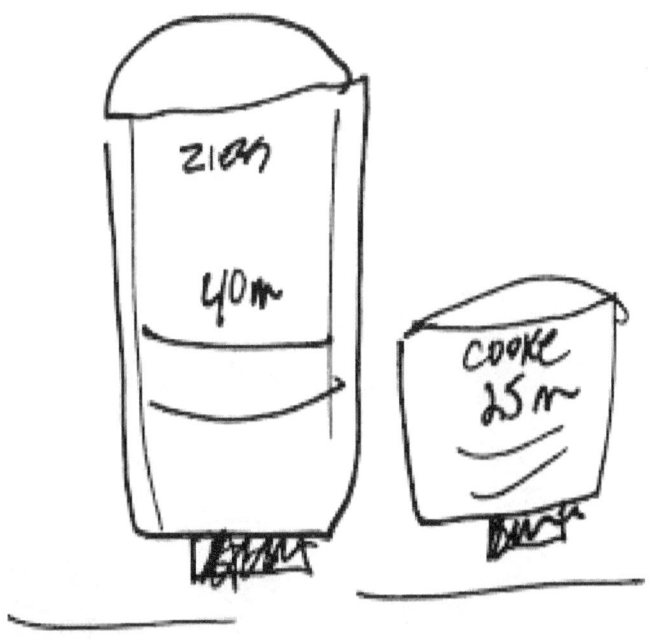

No debates about screen direction.

Figure that out prior to the shoot. And if you don't know, trust the script supervisor and the cinematographer. Make a decision and shoot. Once you allow for an open discussion, everybody starts chiming in. What's next? A forum on what top the actress should wear?

There are so many great technical books that tackle the topic of screen direction and staging. Good shooting boards will solve it.

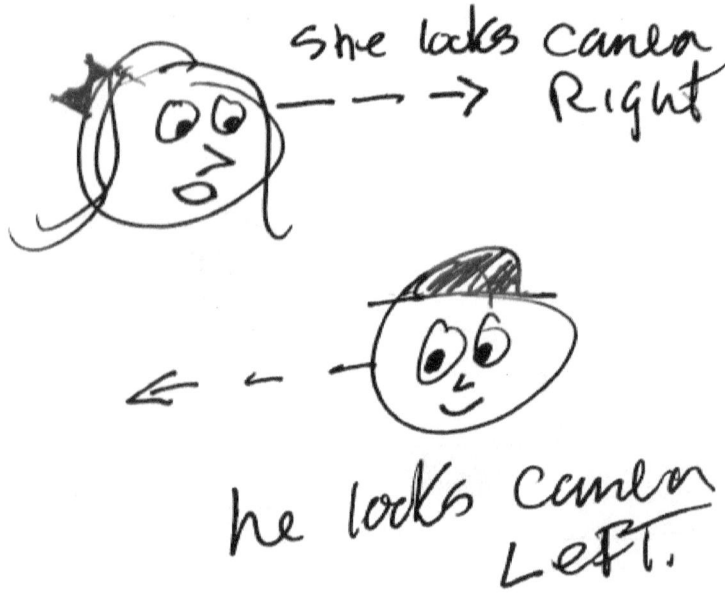

Talk everyone out of the wide shot.

The time the wide shot takes to set up, light and shoot is inversely proportionate to the amount of screen time it gets in the spot. Often there are ugly things around the location too.

Try and dismiss it.

Theater of the mind can be very powerful. We know when we're in a castle, even when we don't see that great establishing shot.

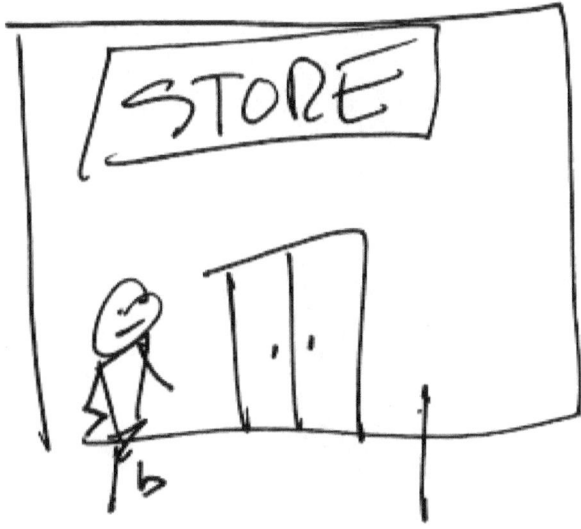

Cheat the reverse.

Instead of moving the camera and lights to the other side of the room to shoot a reverse shot, sometimes you can simply alter the background and have the actor look the proper direction. It's a huge time saver, allowing for more performance in front of the camera.

It helps to change the key light so it matches how the light would play if you did turn everything around to shoot the actual reverse.

We shot the dentist and the Tooth Fairy against the same wall, allowing us to bang out five spots in one day. All by cheating the reverse. We also talked the client out of the wide shot.

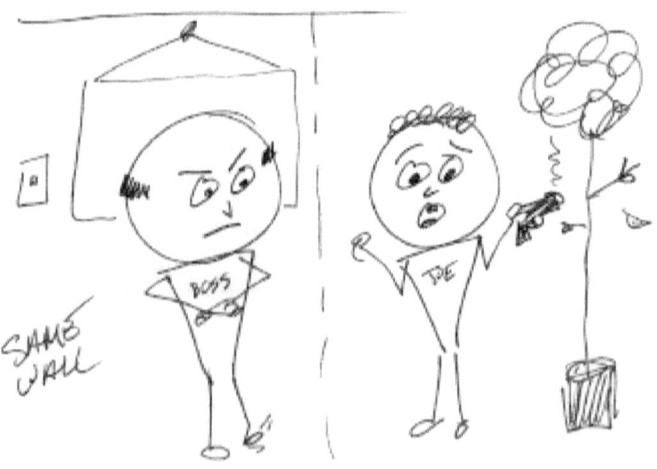

Sports bar test.

When your spot plays at the loud sports bar, with no sound on, will people get it? With great acting, concise visual storytelling and deft editing, yes. Yes they will.

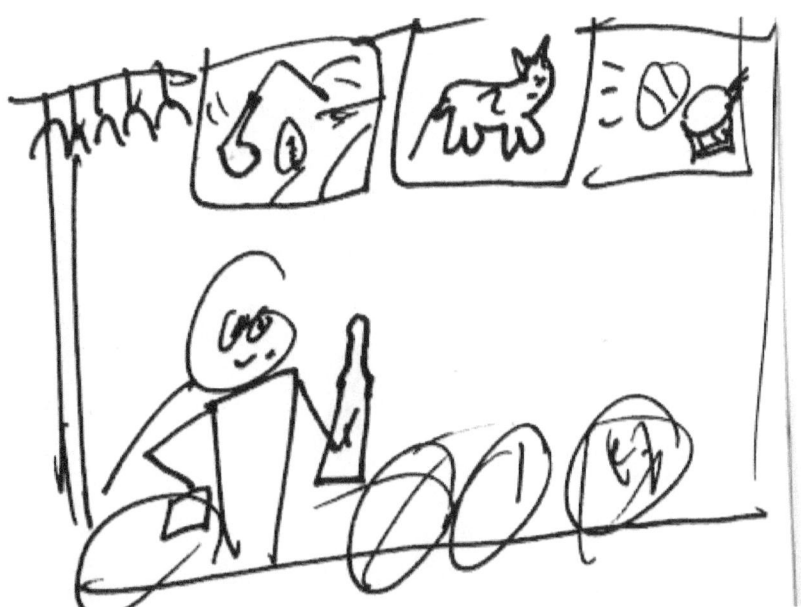

Explain feeling to DP.

When you're starting out, the technical aspects of the camera can be overwhelming. You may not know what lens size conveys the point best. But I bet you know it when you see it. See what you like. So try explaining the mood and vibe you're going for and allow the cinematographer to do her job. Then you can react to choices presented to you. This should happen in prep, then continue on set.

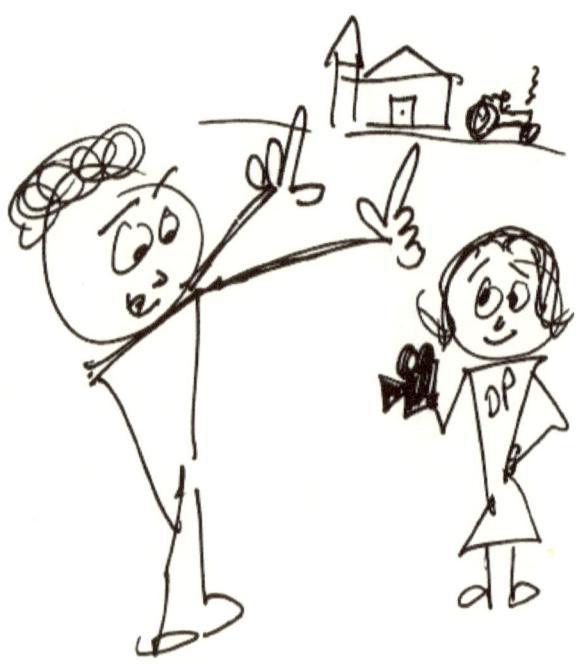

Dirty. Depends.

Dirty shots are when you're shooting over someone's shoulder. I love the look, with the back of an actor's head out of focus in the foreground while we focus on the performer in frame. But it can be constraining in post if the action doesn't quite match. Clean shots are easier to edit, as they are independent of all action.

More importantly, a clean shot of an actor puts us in their head. We share the point of view with that character.

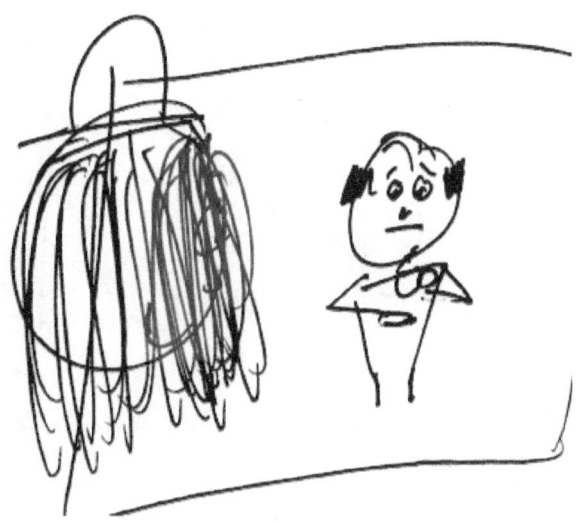

Shoot a cutaway.

It's the same thinking as shooting a reaction shot, but I define a cutaway as anything you can cut to. A clock, cheese plate or the old public address system loudspeaker are all good ones.

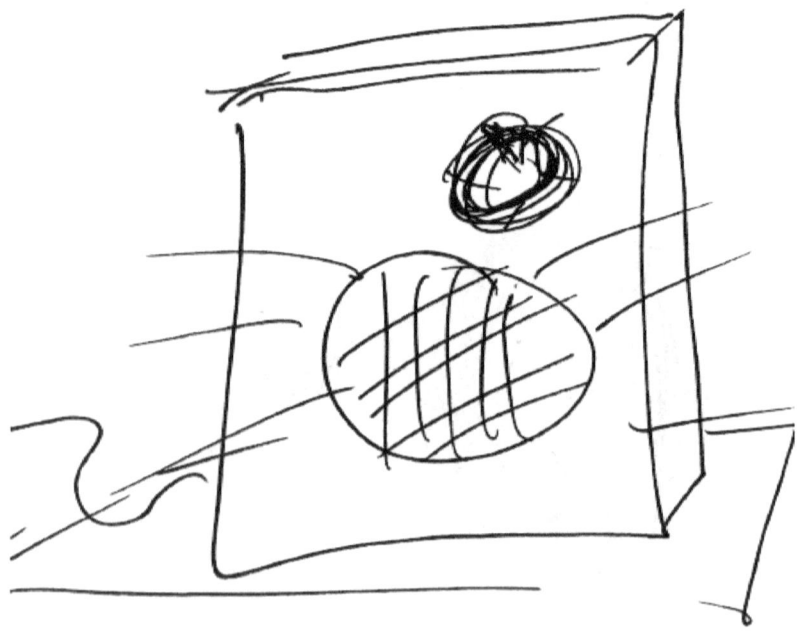

40mm is funniest lens.

The 40mm best mimics the human eye, so I believe it makes us feel like we are part of the scene. Most cinematographers will have a 35mm on set, and that works too. But I like the 40mm.

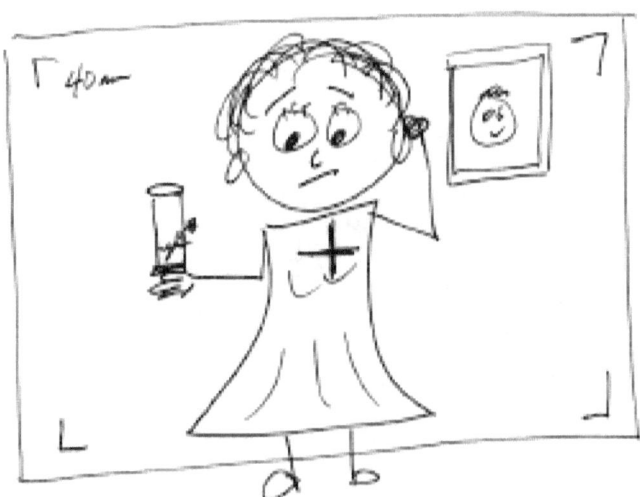

100mm is a sexy lens.

The 100mm compresses the frame and throws the background out of focus, like every restaurant date scene in every romantic comedy. It makes your film footage feel high dollar.

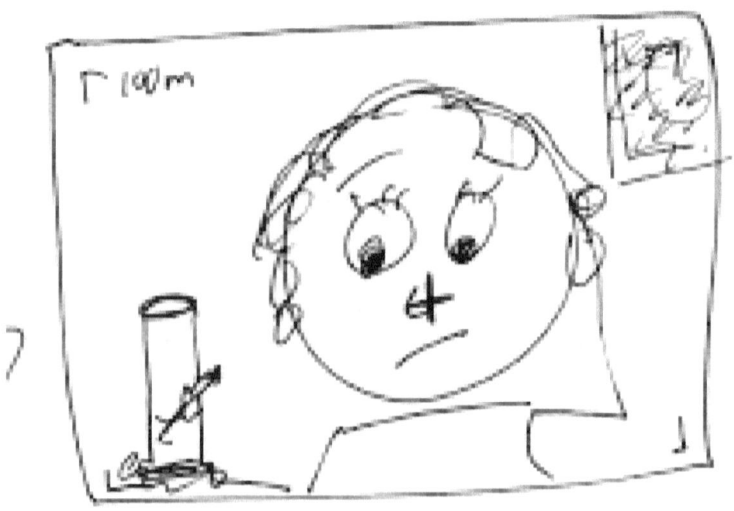

New zooms lens look great & very efficient.

With a fast zoom, you have an infinite variety of focal lengths without having to ever change the lens. I've done entire shoots on the zoom.

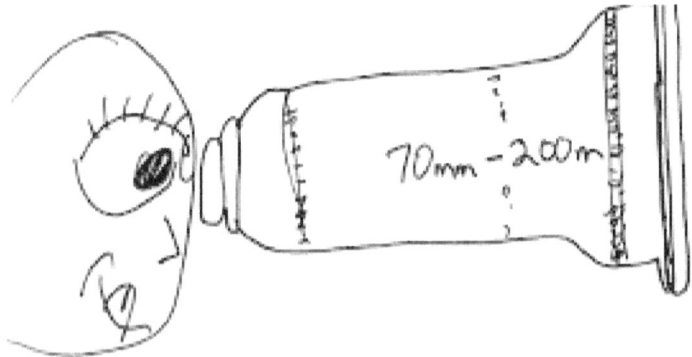

Boom vs. lavaliere microphones.

I like the old school approach of having the sound and dialogue correspond to the camera's perspective. So the sound is more distant in a wide shot, and then more present in the close up shots. Most features are still done this way and it gives a more enhanced aural experience. That's primarily done with the boom mic and delivers a rich, full sound.

Lavaliere microphones have a thinner sound and you get the rustle of the clothes. My pet peeve is seeing that bump under an actor's shirt. Lavs are great life savers in noisy situations.

Personally, I try and only use the boom, but sometimes use both the boom and the lavalieres simultaneously and lean heavy on the boom in the mix.

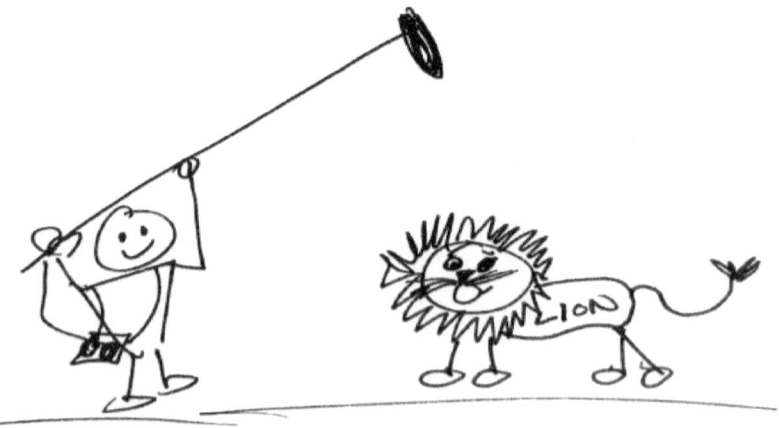

Don't start with the wide shot.

When I must do a wide shot of a scene, I avoid starting the shoot day with that. Why? After a sluggish start to get that first shot off, the agency or client or you can fixate on details of the scene that will end up on the cutting room floor.

I prefer to start with a shot that gets the crew going and gets the team momentum rolling. It sets a nice pace for the day.

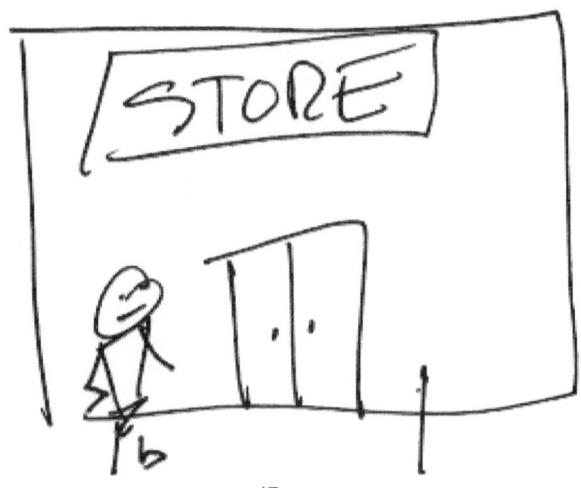

Schedule around the performances.

Performance is key. Consider if your talent or subject or stunt is better delivering their best for you at a certain time of the day and build the shoot around that. It's not always about what is easiest or even logical. Make it about the best time to capture the meat of the spot.

If your leading lady is going to look a little tired late in the day, try to shoot her close up sooner. While she's in make up, grab other reactions and cutaways that are simple but vital.

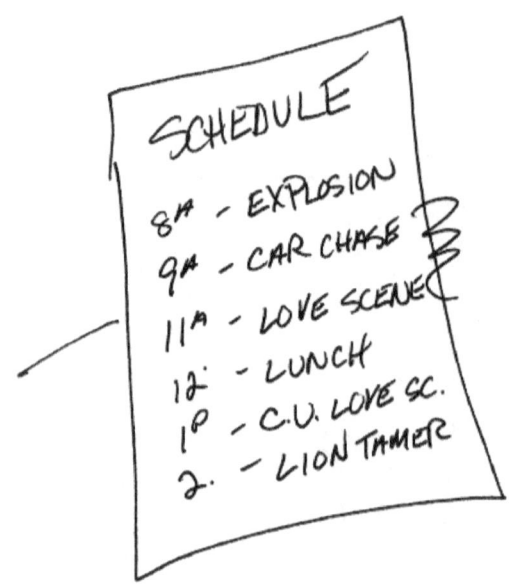

Product shot first.

No one in the business agrees with me, except clients. They love this. Clients often care most about how their product is filmed, and have experience on set with how it is lit and framed. They've also seen film crews push it to the end of the day, the thinking being while the big equipment is being wrapped, we bang out the product shot. I feel this is disrespectful to the client.

Give the product shot all the love and focus earlier in the shoot day, and the client will be chill and happy. I've had clients leave set and fly home. "You've got what I need, and I trust you with the comedy. See you next time."

Respect that the burger, shoe or juice is paying for the spot.

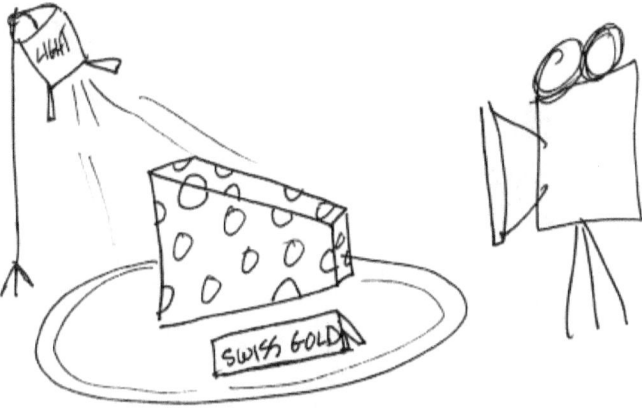

Kids close up first.

I retrofit a kid's performance from his or her medium close up, to the wide shot. Meaning, I do the wide shot after the great takes we already got in the closer shots where it counts. Kids can burn out, so get the good stuff in the tighter shots.

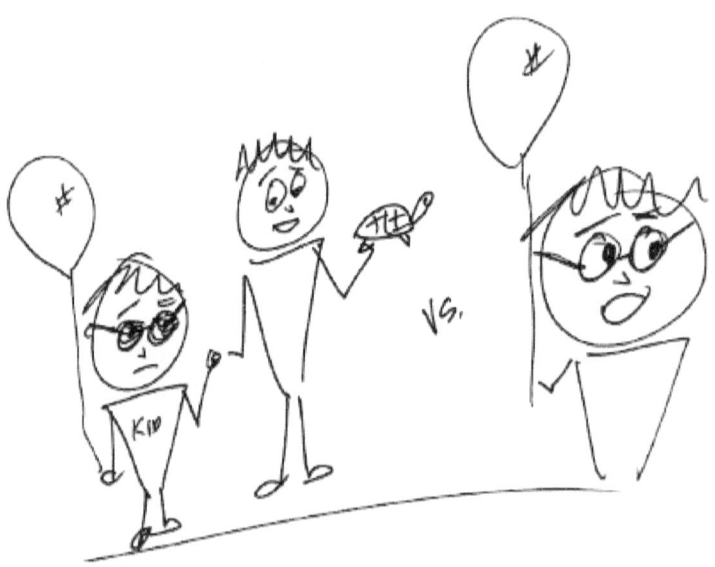

50-50 and tail slate.

It's a secret term that tells the crew we are rolling the camera but do not want the actors to know. Like during a rehearsal when you don't want any pressure on the actors, you can call "50-50" and you'll get a relaxed performance. Now, the entire crew needs to know the term, not just the camera department. These days, many younger people on the crew do not know it. Tell them.

Tail-slating a shot is hitting the clapper at the end, usually it is held upside down and the editor sees it and syncs the sound.

You'll love using the 50-50 technique with kids or even with non-actors, and occasionally less-seasoned performers that are nervous once they get on set with a large crew around them.

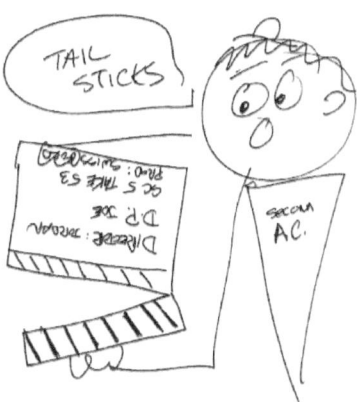

Kids can parrot you.

Sit next to the camera and literally have the child actor mimic you. Tell them, "pretend you are a parrot and say what I say, exactly like I say it," like a game! Then feed them their lines and any alternate lines you want to get. It works with grown ups too, just leave out the "pretend you're a parrot" part.

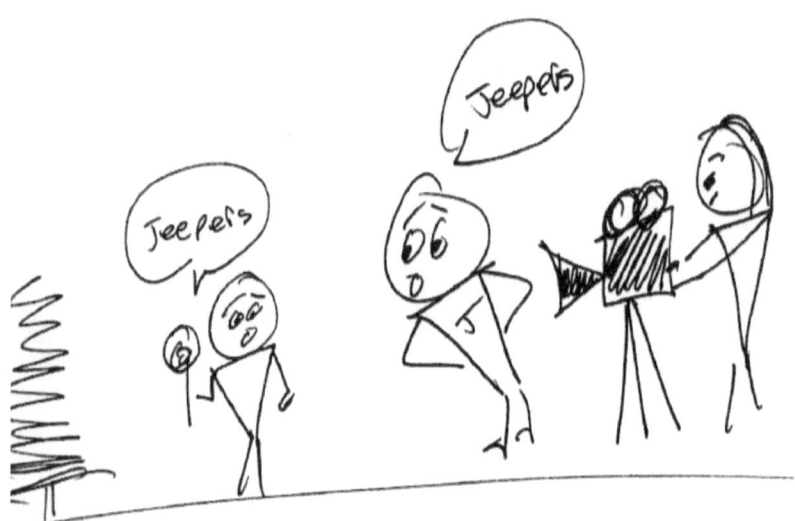

Kids split screen.

Say you have two kids on a couch talking, you can shoot them one a time and marry the performances in post through simple split screen technology. I've sat on the left of frame and had a kid parrot me, then sat on the right of frame for the other kid.

It helps to lock off the camera. You can always add a hand held movement in post after you've joined the takes together.

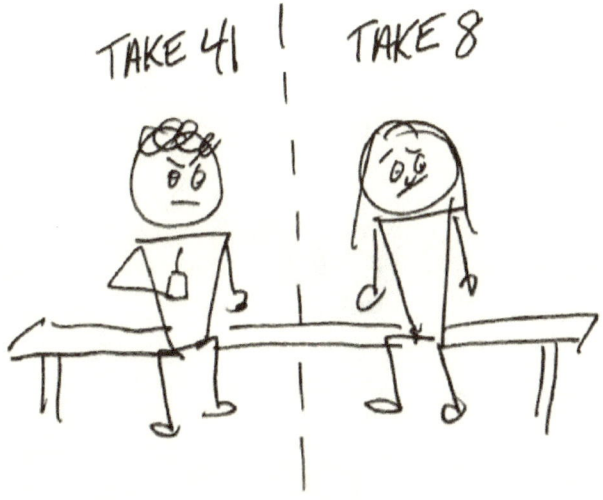

Learn to say "cut!"

In this digital era, it's too easy to let the camera roll while you do take after take. After all, it's just 1's and 0's and hard drive space is cheap. But consider the editor combing through eleven takes on one media clip. She may not get to that last gem. Or worse, decide there is no real difference among the several takes, so he stops looking after take five.

Once I have a great take in a series like that, I'll say "cut" with authority. Then I'll do one more take slated so it becomes a sole, independent media clip. This last take is exactly how the performers just did it, so the editor sees it.

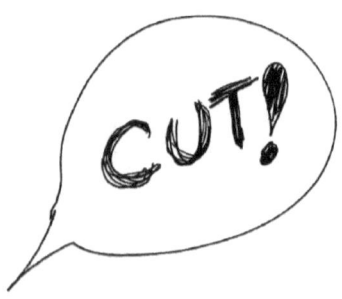

Allow crew to work.

I find film crew members strive to do their best work, so let them. Grab some veggies from the craft service table and go discuss how great things are going with your advertising agency team in the video village. (Also see: Snack while lighting.)

You hate when people breathe down your neck. Some things take time. So show some respect and give your talented group of men and women on the crew a little space to work.

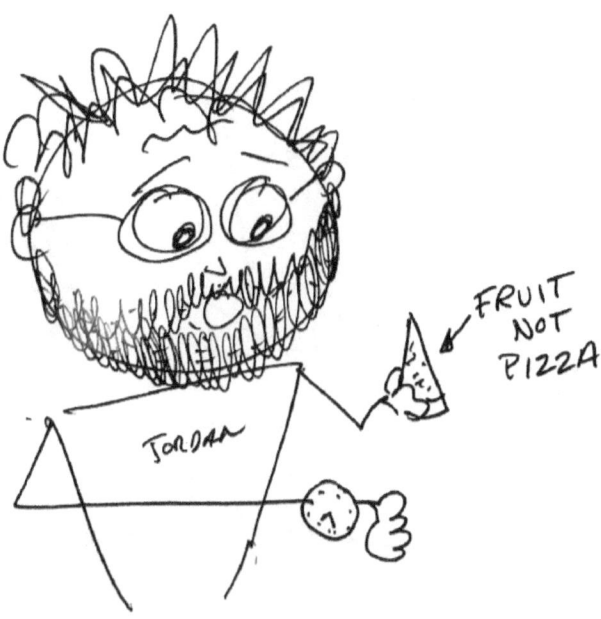

Be Zen & in charge.

Stay chill. The era of yelling and berating people are gone. You can lead with a firm and decisive hand without being a dick.

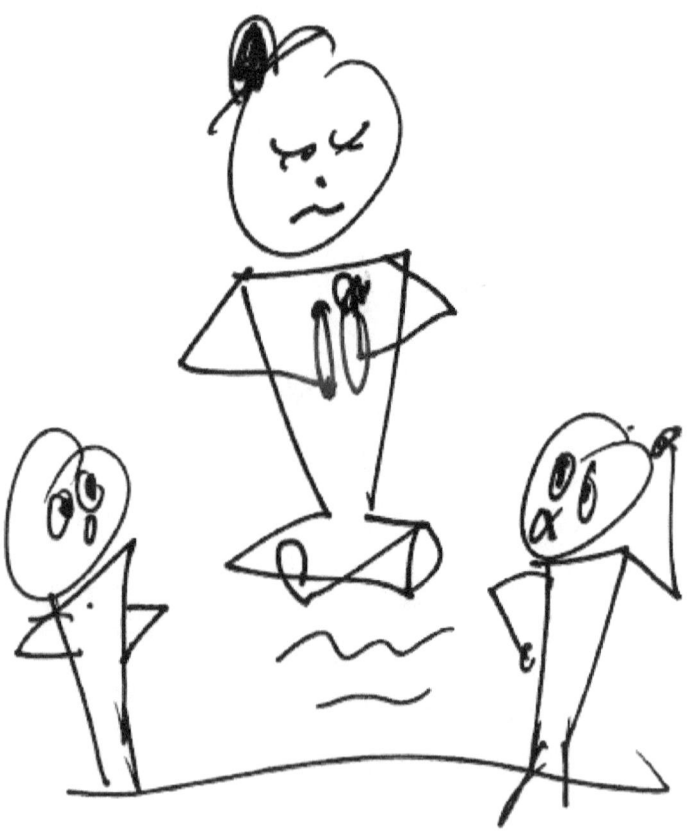

Humor is your friend.

Coming from a stand-up comedy background, humor is a tool I love to use to keep things fun. But you don't need to be a nightclub comedian to keep your sense of humor about things. We're not saving a life on the operating table, we are selling a product.

I used to be too funny on set! Looking back, I may have given the impression that I was not taking the gig seriously enough. Luckily, the end results quelled such suspicions.

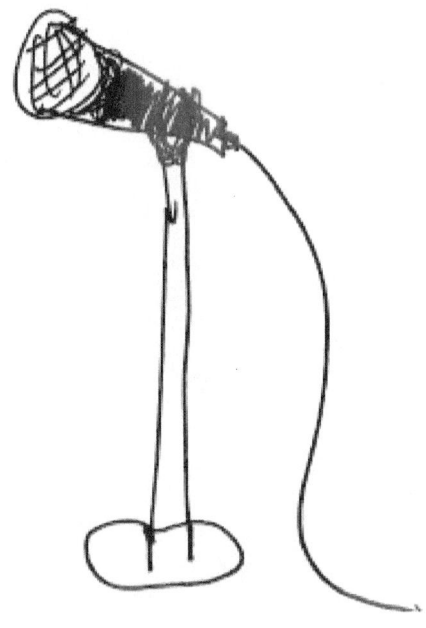

Shoot in the rain?

Producer-types will tell you to go ahead and shoot in the rain, and that the rain is not really noticeable on camera. Sometimes that is true. I fear when the creative team gets into post and the sky is crappy and the rain hits here and there, I'll be thrown under the bus. "How could he shoot in the rain?" Such a tough call, you hate to sit around, but if you can postpone a little bit, maybe that sun may just come out. Now you've got a free wet down for that high dollar look!

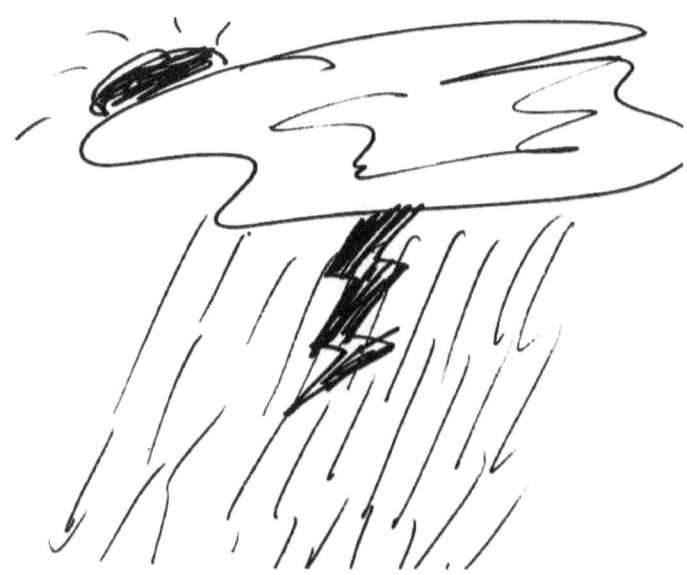

Make your actors feel special.

Actors are truly amazing. First of all, I mean really c'mon, how do they remember all those lines? They are special and bring the words to life. Don't fraternize too much and allow them their space, and appreciate all that they contribute.

I've heard stories of actors barely talking with the Director, and that any comments were relayed via the 1st AD all day! Wow, those Directors are shorting themselves a great opportunity to collaborate with wonderful artists, even on a soap commercial.

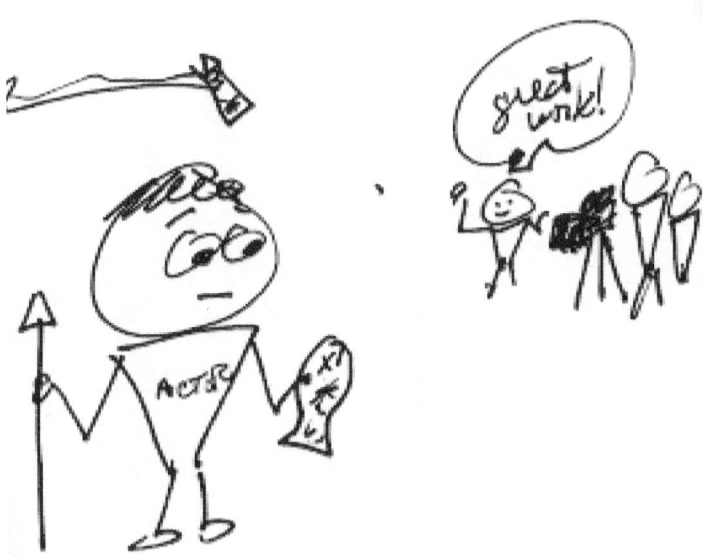

Make your clients feel special.

Don't fraternize too much, but respect that these folks are trusting you with their brand. Be sincere in your appreciation. Many Brand Managers have marketing degrees or agency experience, so they know a thing or two. Some attend more shoots than you.

Respect what the clients bring to the table, while remembering that you work for the advertising agency. Once a client asked if we could significantly change some set decoration. While I saw nothing wrong with his innocent request, my answer was "let's go talk with the agency."

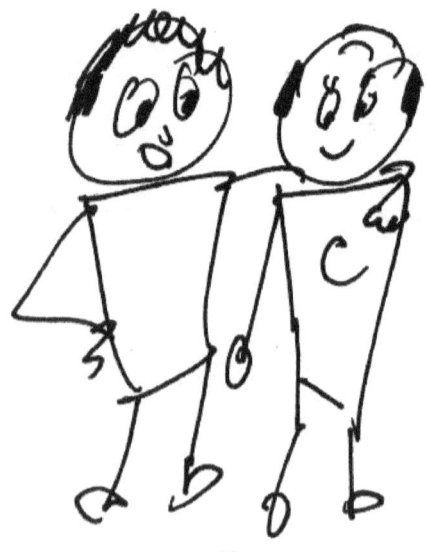

Make your agency feel special.

They are! They came up with the campaign, darn it. Keep the agency in the loop and appreciate the long, arduous road they've taken to get to the shoot. As a commercial director, I am basically a midwife. The agency and the client got pregnant and I am to deliver this campaign. But they'll take it and raise it once the afterbirth is cleaned up.

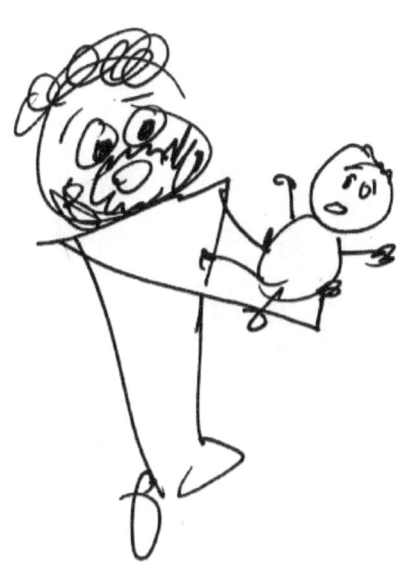

No chit-chatters around camera.

Don't let people talk around the camera. Often hair and make up artists sit nearby so to be at-the-ready, but they'll carry on whispering conversations. Politely tell them to not talk so you can focus. Even the grips and electricians who've all worked ferociously to get you able to shoot can be chit chatters. No talking before and during takes. It is unacceptable. The sole reason we gather is to capture a magic moment on film. Shh.

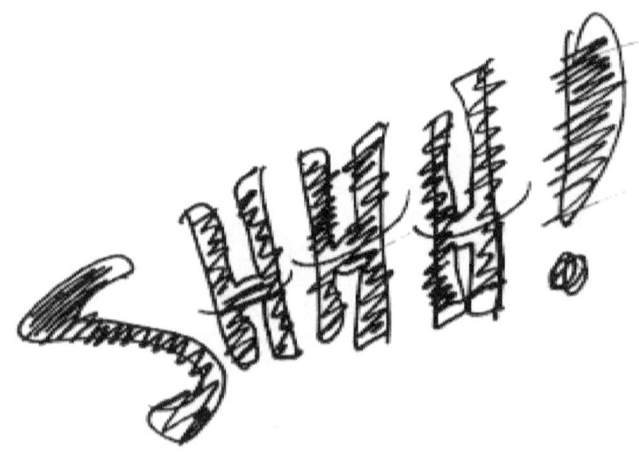

The fish stinks from the head down.

You set the tone of your set. Don't be a dick.

There are only solutions in filmmaking.

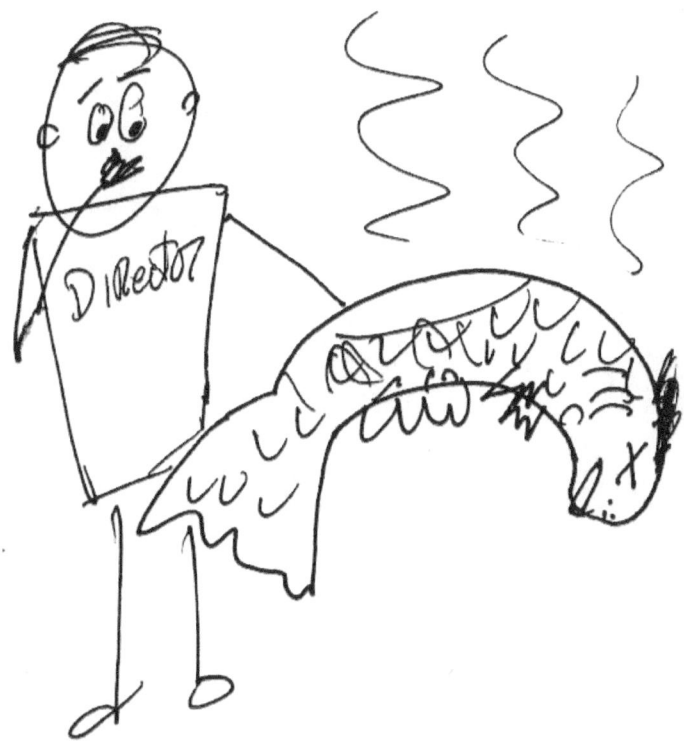

Ten-minute warning.

I'll announce this to the crew when I am getting antsy: "Tense up everyone, we're ten minutes away from our first shot, so wrap up your conversations. If it doesn't pertain to this shoot, let's abort that chit chat altogether. Thank you."

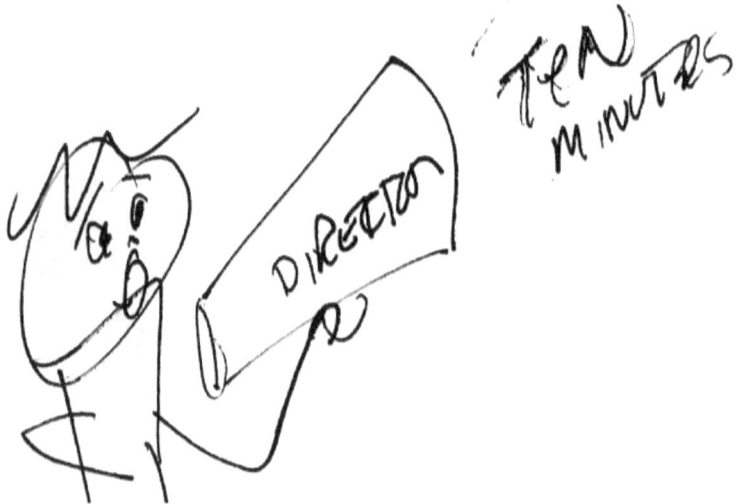

Block. Light. Rehearse.

It may sound obvious, yet so many filmmakers do not take the time to block a scene or rehearse the actors. I find the quick blocking so valuable for every department. Actors know what we're doing, sound knows how to boom the shoot, the focus puller can get marks. It's been the process for over one hundred years. Maybe there is a reason why?

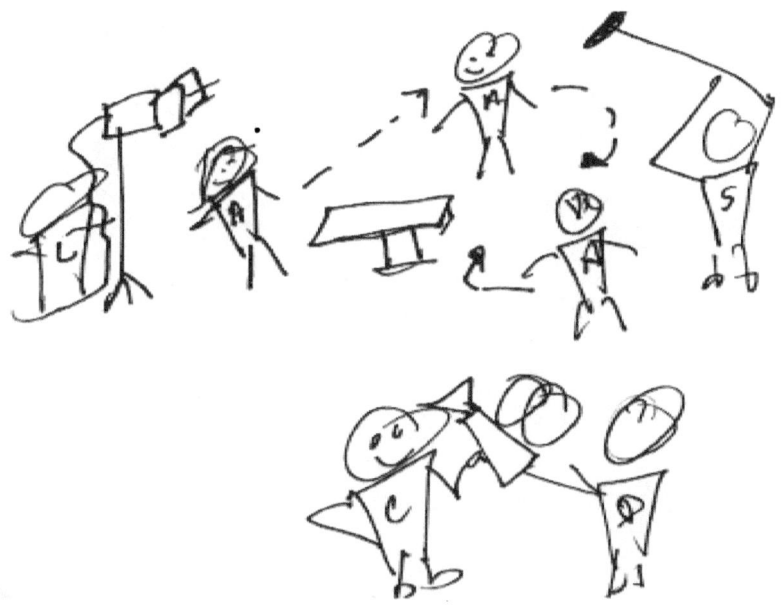

Shoot the rehearsal.

Sometimes the situation is ready to go without the need to do major blocking, or your team needs to get the momentum going for the day. In that case, shoot the rehearsal. Just make sure you won't be embarrassed if that take makes it into the spot.

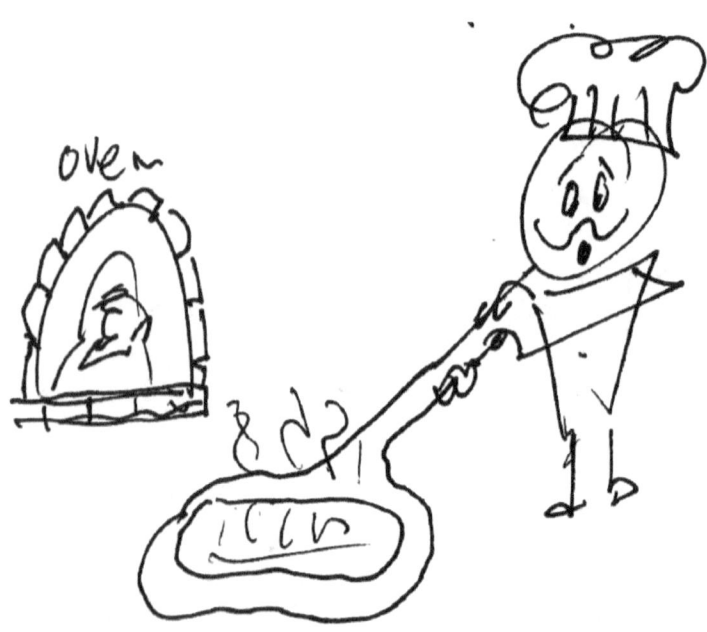

Actors like verbs.

"Be suspicious of her."
"Dismiss him when he mentions his solution."
"Flirt with the detergent."

I try to give specific verbs to my actors and then allow them to interpret that.

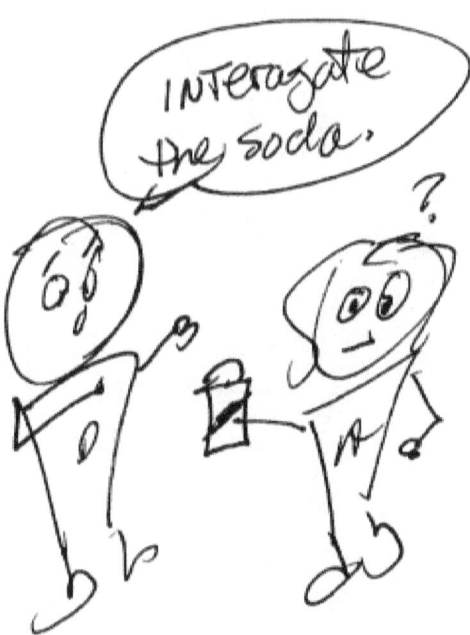

The silent take.

If you have the actors do the scene without speaking any of the dialogue, that may prove useful for reactions. For more dramatic material, this method can stir up some great emotions that will convey the point of the scene without words.

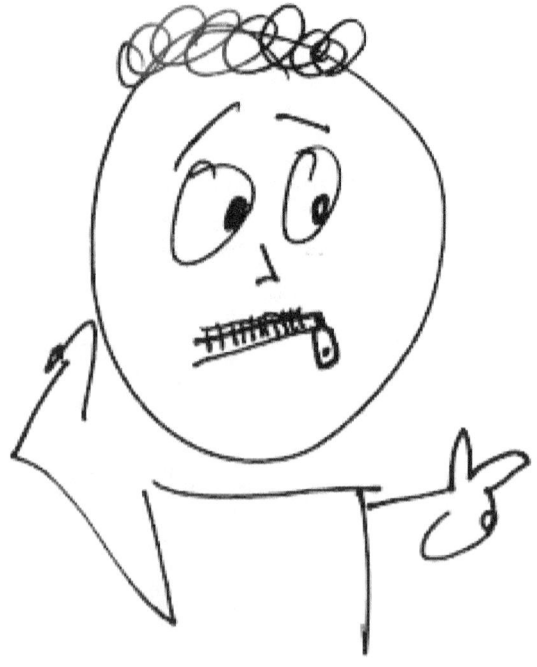

Play the reality of the absurdity.

When a situation is already funny, the actors should not try to be funny. Instead, they need to believe in the scenario and treat it as their character's reality.

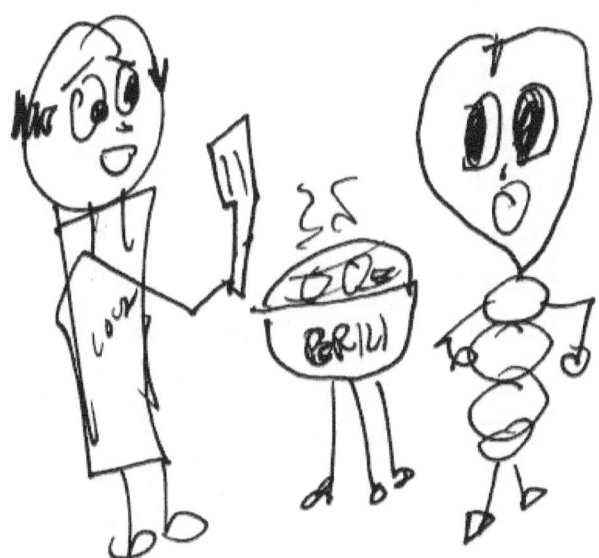

Funny before lunch.

10am to noon is the sweet spot to capture comedy. After lunch, there is a sluggishness in the cast and crew as they digest.

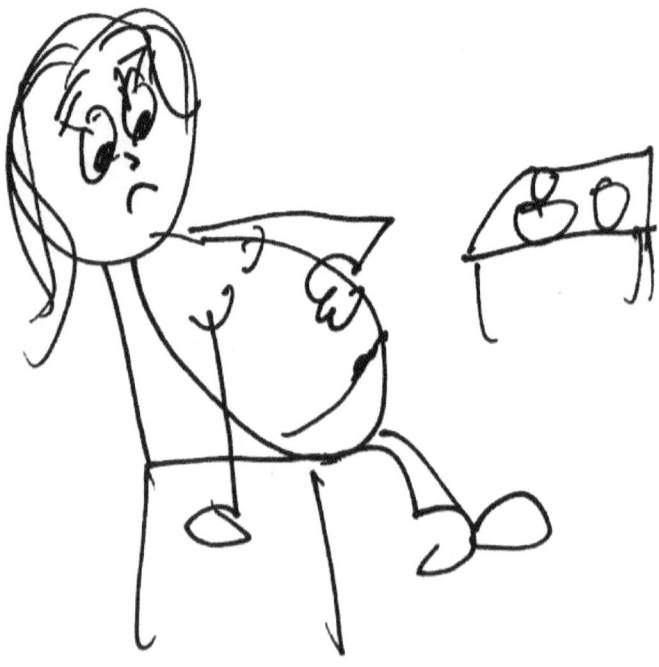

Fresh breath after lunch.

I demand mints, individual dental flossers, gum and sometimes even mouthwash be passed around at the end of lunch. To crew, client and anyone on set. Fresh breath gives us dignity and makes life better. Oh, have a mini trash can for the flossers so they don't end up on the ground.

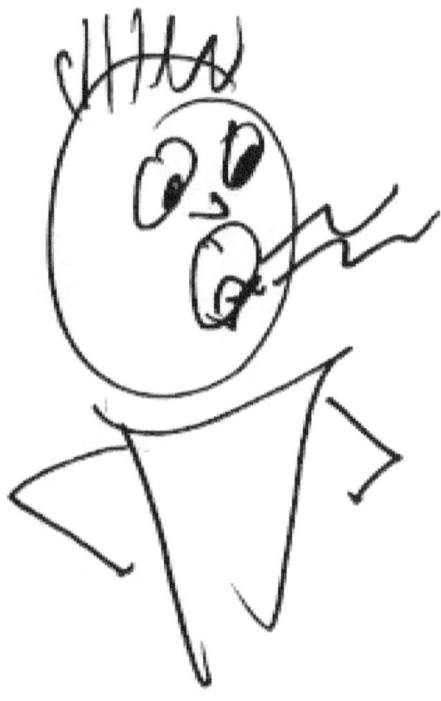

Poor Man's Process.

This is when you film a moving car without moving the car. Instead you move lights and shake the camera slightly to give the illusion of traveling. There are great YouTube videos featuring notable filmmakers doing it. Take the seven minutes to learn it. Works best at night and with fake rain.

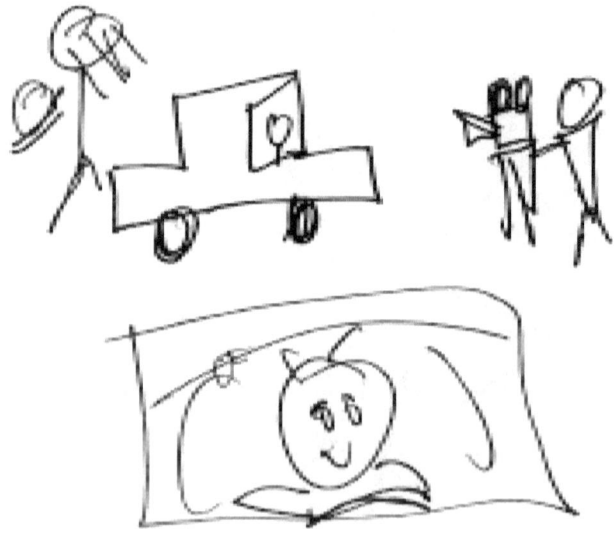

"Is there time for that in the cut?"

I hate to poo poo any good idea, but when a bad idea is so bad that you can't even muster the strength to tell the passionate, extremely creative person just how lame that idea is, just say:

"Is there time in the cut for that shot? I don't believe there is. Darn. Rrrrr." And then shake your fist to the heavens.

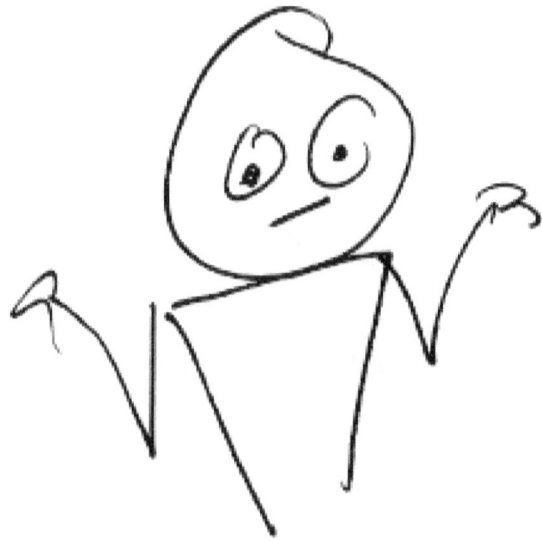

You & me should be sipping cocktails...

As an actor, I did a fast food spot for a burger, and the Director told me I nailed after the fifth take! "If it were up to me, we would be sipping cocktails at the beach..." Then he leaned in and confessed, "but the client over there has a problem with the way you're saying 'fast food', so let's do a few takes where you make it sound like fast food is awesome." He rolled his eyes as if to say how crazy the note was. "Hey, I know we got it. Just humor them." Then he mimed sipping that cocktail.

Fifteen takes later, we had it. That director made a pre-emptive move to keep me relaxed, knowing how the client was particular.

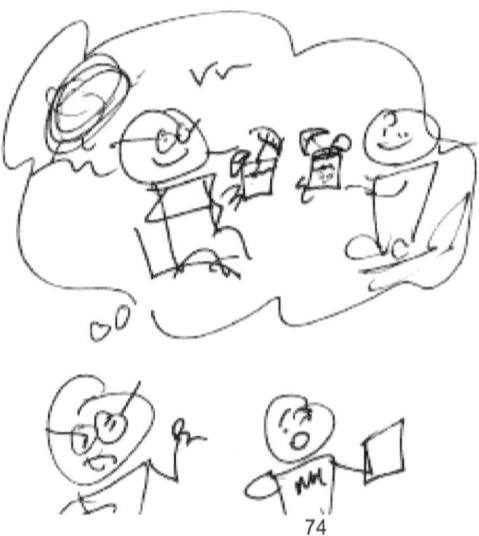

Any which way you want to do it.

Giving the actor a take where they can do whatever they wish with the line typically yields a very relaxed performance and can ease nerves. It shows you're here to play a bit and value their contributions.

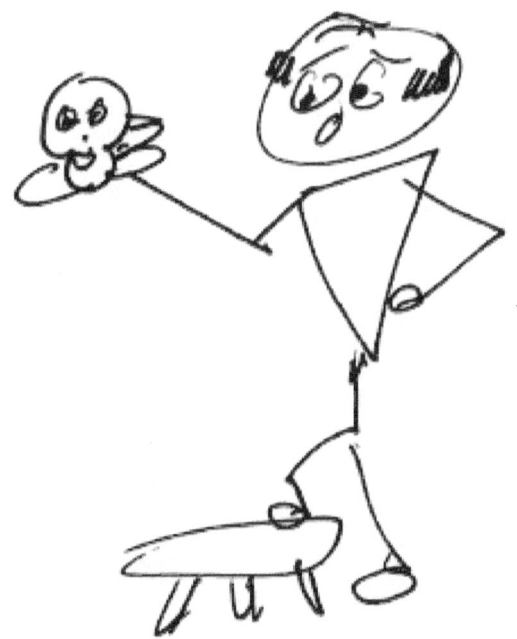

Meet non-actors first.

Directors Stacy Peralta, Tony Franklin and my lovely and very talented wife are the masters of getting great interviews in their documentary spots. Jeannette Godoy meets her subjects and informs them of what they'll be talking about. She warns them she'll be processing some of the answers so not to be alarmed by any silent moments in the process.

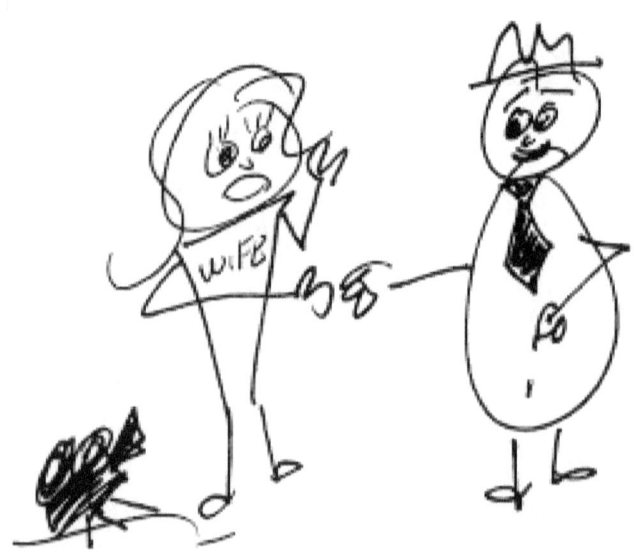

Play dumb & re-frame.

In my docu work, I act like I am really slow to understand what a subject's answer means, then ask them to explain it one more time. My director of photographer knows to use this repeated answer as a second take, and she'll zoom in to give me editorial options. Now I can cut the answer together and make it succinct.

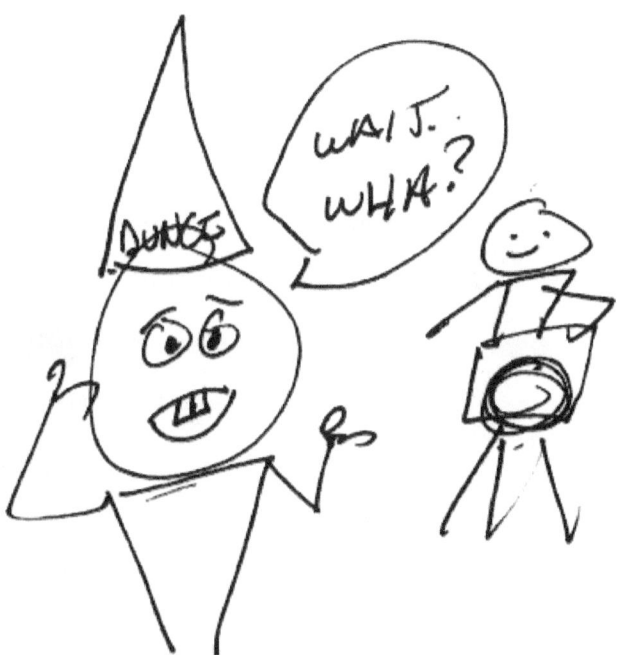

Beware of the drones.

Drones can take a lot of time away from shooting. You better know just what is the piece of the footage that will end up in the final spot. They've also become so ubiquitous that it's like, "oh you had a drone." Can you get the same shot faster off a twelve step ladder?

Just like a Steady-cam shot, know your in and out points, utilize the tool for your specific needs and move on. I've sent the drone team home after thirty minutes because they delivered and were no longer needed.

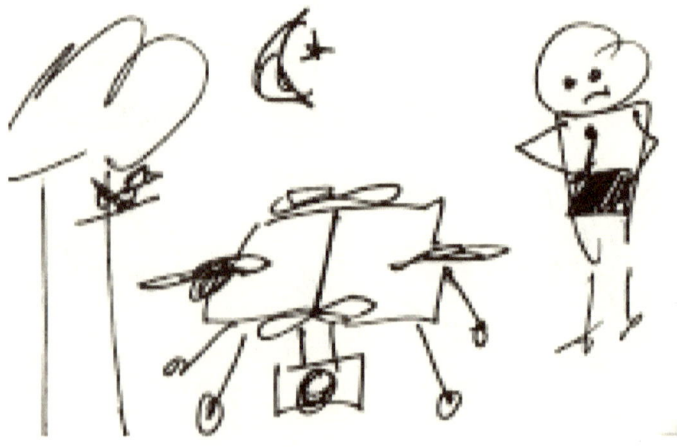

Embrace the drones.

Drones are freakin' cool and offer shots you could never before obtain. A well-placed drone shot can truly add major production value. Just board the shot first.

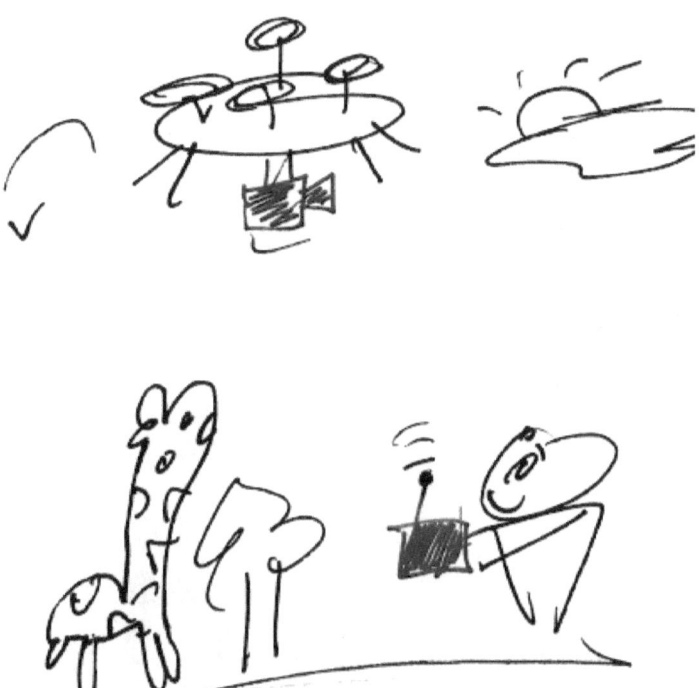

Slower is the new faster.

Too many times, when people rush to set up a shot somebody drops something or worse someone gets hurt. Then everything comes to a halt. Slow down, take a breath. Slow but steady wins the shoot.

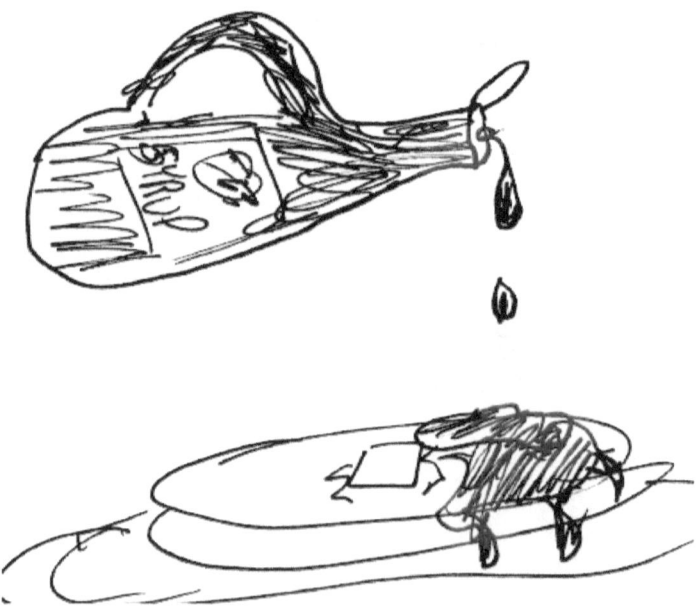

It's never about money.

Once I say yes to a project, I pour 120% of my soul into making it the best project, regardless of the pay or budget. I hate when I overhear, "Hey, I'm only getting paid half my rate." Screw your rate. You need to listen to that little bird named Integrity as she sings her sweet song, also called, "Integrity."

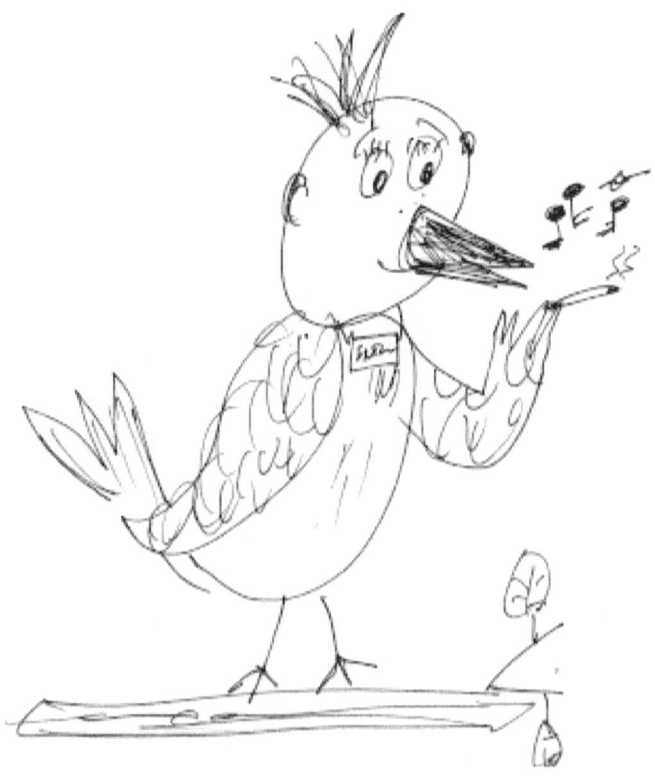

Don't help wrap.

OK, maybe if you're on a boat. Otherwise, let the crew do their job. Each department has a certain way they wrap their gear and you're just getting in the way. I once had a production assistant tell me, "Please stop helping, sir. I want your job someday and when I get there, I don't want to be helping wrap, so I don't want to see you doing it now. Thanks."

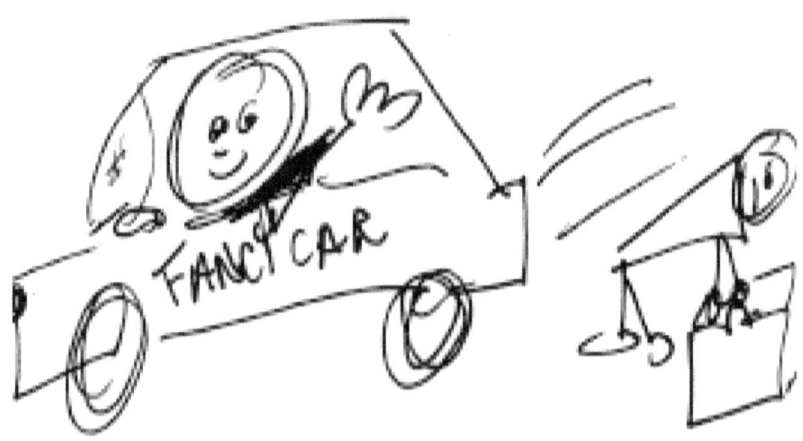

Say thank you.

Offering a sincere "thank you" to your crew is the right thing to do. I believe humility and strong leadership are not mutually exclusive.

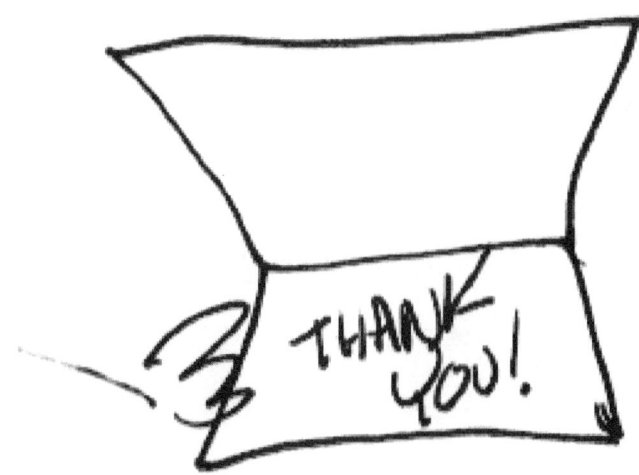

Leave with hard drive.

I leave with a copy of the footage so I can speak about specific takes and eventually perhaps do my own Director's cut for my reel.

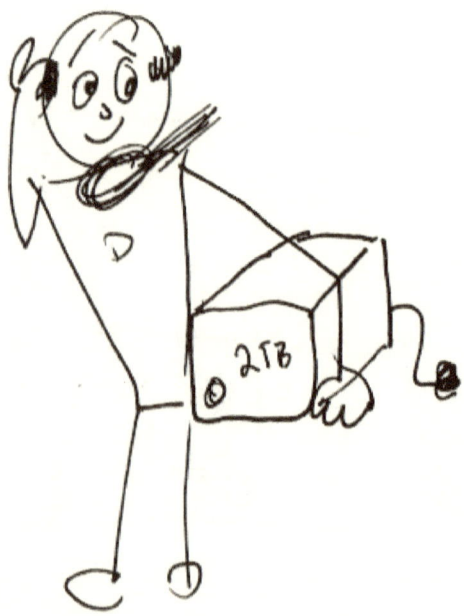

Talk to the editor.

An email downloading what you were going for is very helpful to the editor, even if she has not seen the footage yet. Some editors like to work void of any info, and if that's the case, cool. After all, most editors working in commercials are very talented, and very collaborative. Most also love to glean whatever insights they can from you. Maybe there was a favorite shot or take the entire team was diggin' on set. Convey that.

Many friendly, professional editors will ask if they can help you do a Director's Cut for your reel. Help them make the best spot for the agency, and let them help you with your Director's Cut.

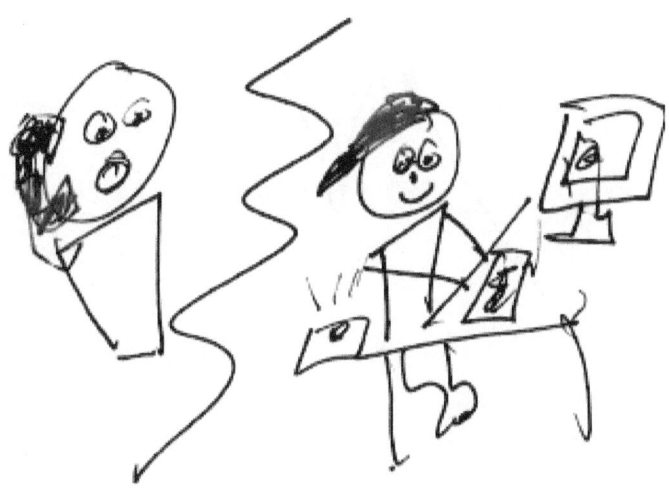

Be ruthless in the edit.

Don't fall in love with a shot just because it took an hour to set up, or used a cool toy. If it doesn't move the story along, chuck it. If no one else is getting it, but you swear it is the best thing since the opening of "Goodfellas", maybe you need to step back for a sec.

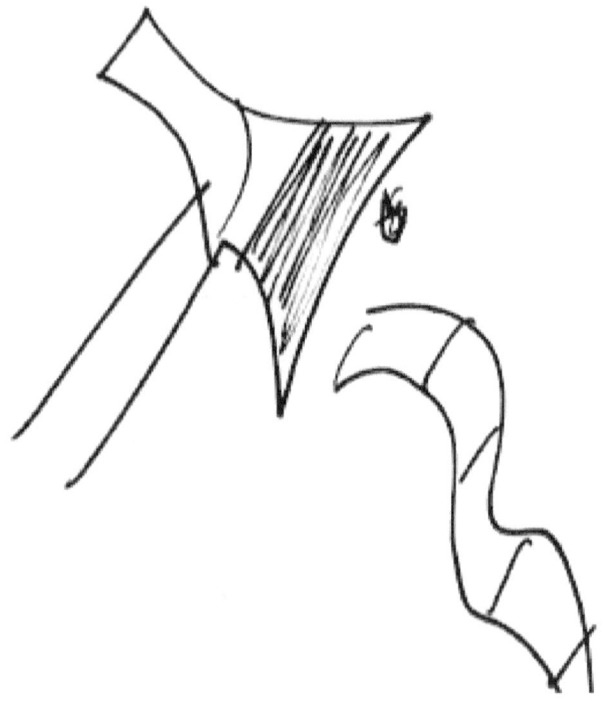

Always think about your reel.

Trust your gut when it comes to your reel. If you know in your heart of hearts a combination of shots work, for example, do a Director's Cut and step away from the process. Some shots won't fit in the on-air cut to make room for some 99-cent offer bullshit. Fine. They client gets what they need to sell tacos and you have your reel. By the way, the agency creatives may want a copy of your cut for their reel.

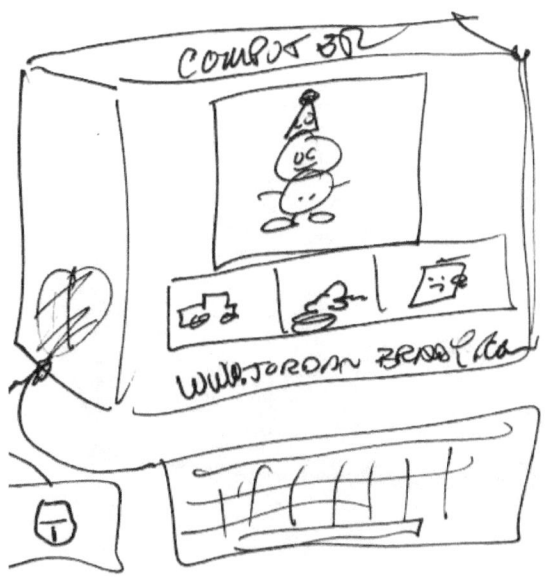

Always tell the truth.

Remember the golden rule and tell the truth. An agency Art Director asked me why a set up was taking longer than expected. I replied, "because I didn't plan the shot properly." Agency people are smart and can sniff out bullshit a mile away. Show them and yourself the respect of being honest.

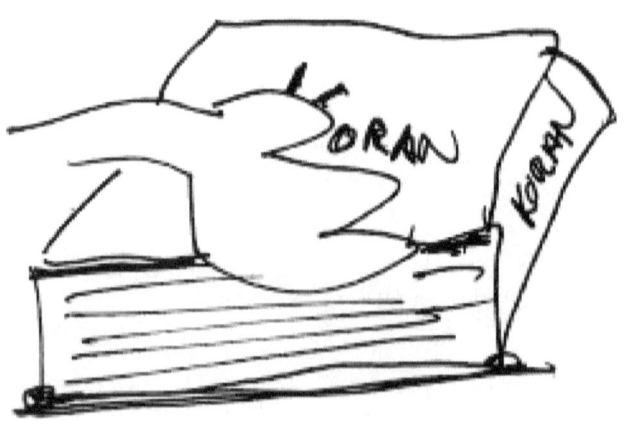

Lie about the budget.

Never tell a soul you shot that epic spot for $800 with your pals. If someone asks, just say you can't put a price on it because of all the favors you called in. Or ask, "how much does it look like we spent?"

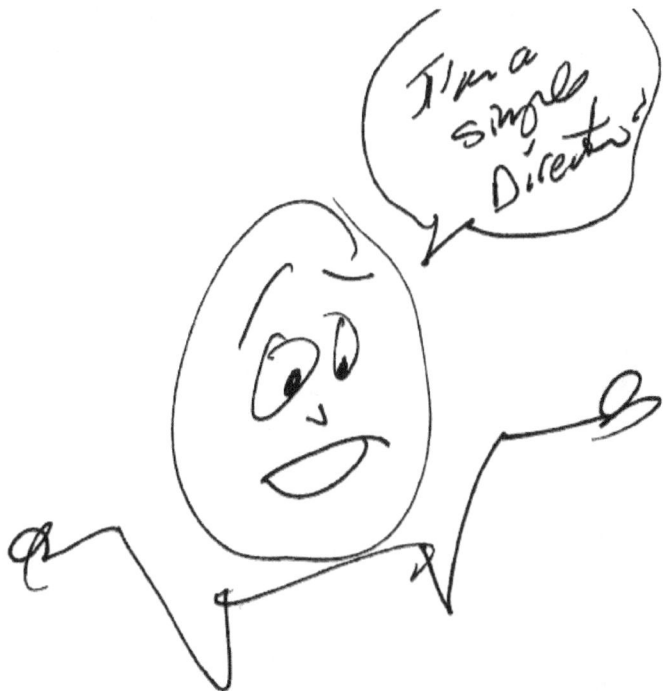

The Power of "no thank you."

Realize you are not right for every project. It was hard to admit that my friend had a more appropriate reel, one that spoke to this potential job. But boy did it felt great when he booked the gig off my recommendation. I try to consider myself a resource for other talented filmmakers. Not to get all trippy, but I believe that goodwill will come back around someday.

As you move through your illustrious career, you and you alone will define your "brand" as we say. Now hopefully, your brand is synonymous with your strong character and sense of integrity.

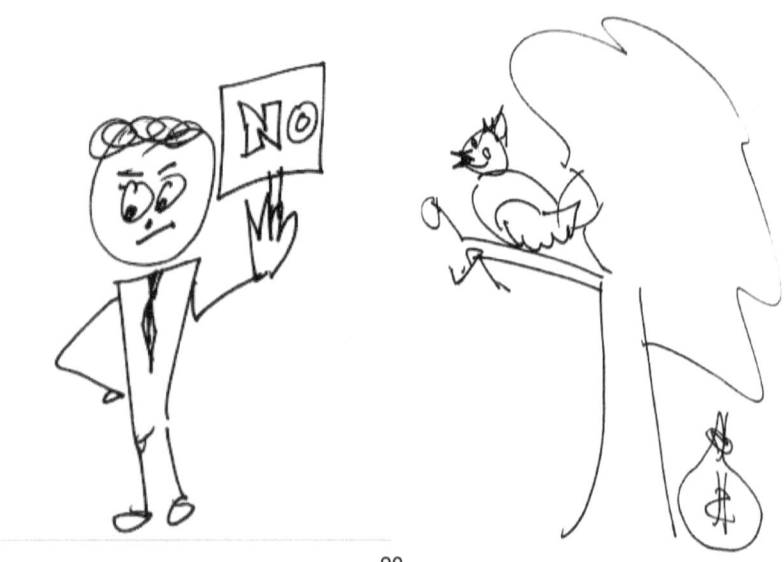

Passion projects.

We each understand that commercials are a balance of art and commerce. So it is of utmost importance you also pursue your personal passion projects outside of work for hire stuff. Short films, art projects, features or say, your volunteer work helping others creatively. You owe it to yourself to stretch artistically. And face it, who doesn't love indulging in any endeavor with complete control?

My documentaries are creative palette cleansers for me. I have final cut, have carved out a small niche and have such fun diving into the unknown. And with the latest film, "I Am Battle Comic", we raised over $30,000 for charities helping military families and veterans.

My complete trilogy on stand-up comedians, "I Am Comic", "I Am Road Comic" and "I Am Battle Comic" are all on iTunes. Links are always at jordanbrady.com to all my stuff.

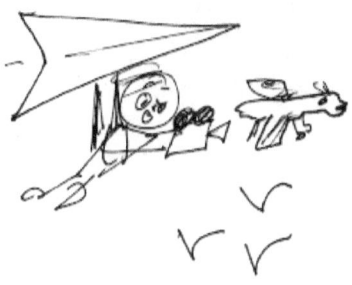

Respect The Process.

A lot of talented people contribute to the making of a successful commercial. Commercial directors tend to reap much of the praise. Just know you cannot do it alone. Many methods have a basis in trial and error, so respect what is proven to work.

Sometime you must subvert the process, so go ahead, be daring and break the rules. You can still respect the people involved, helping you achieve your goals.

"Respect The Process" is also the name of my wildly popular filmmaking podcast on iTunes, Stitcher and jordanbrady.com.

Thank you and I wish you all the success you can dream.

Have fun!

Jordan

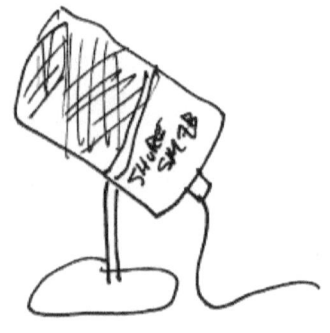

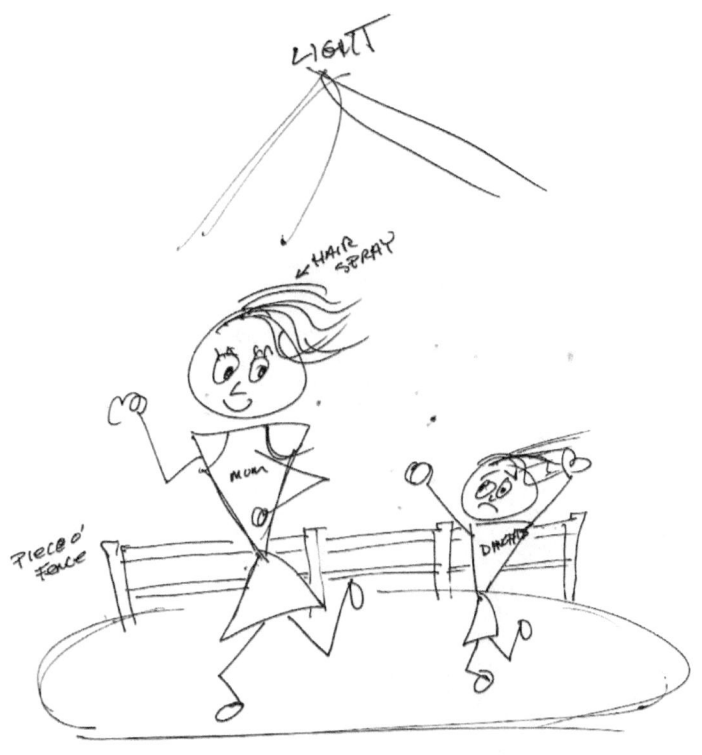

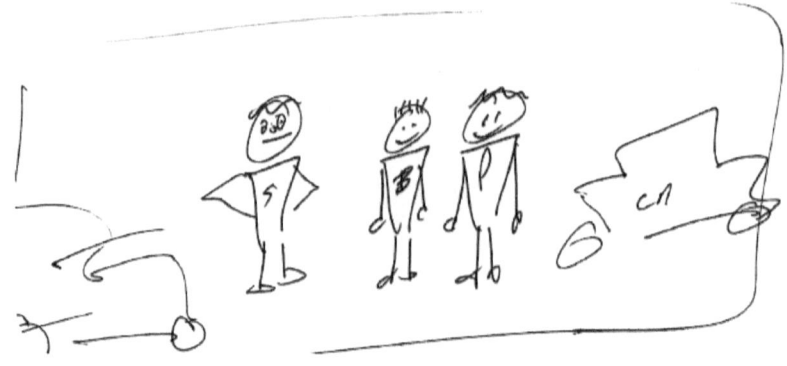
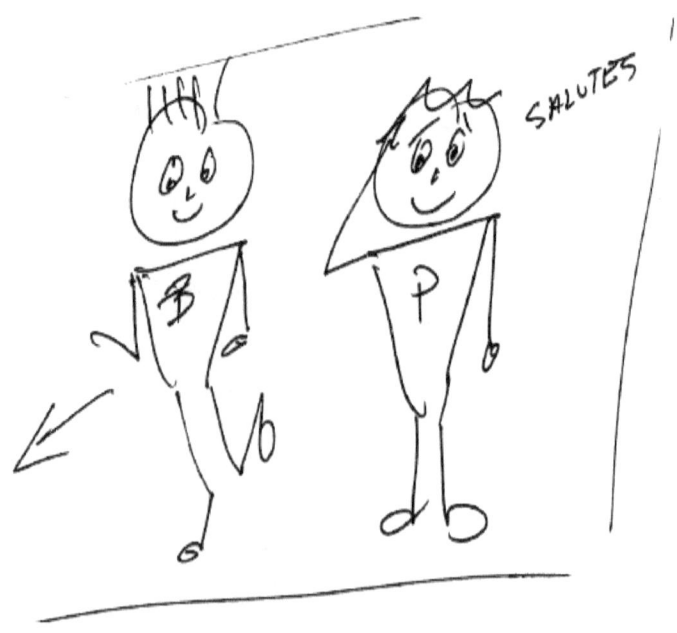

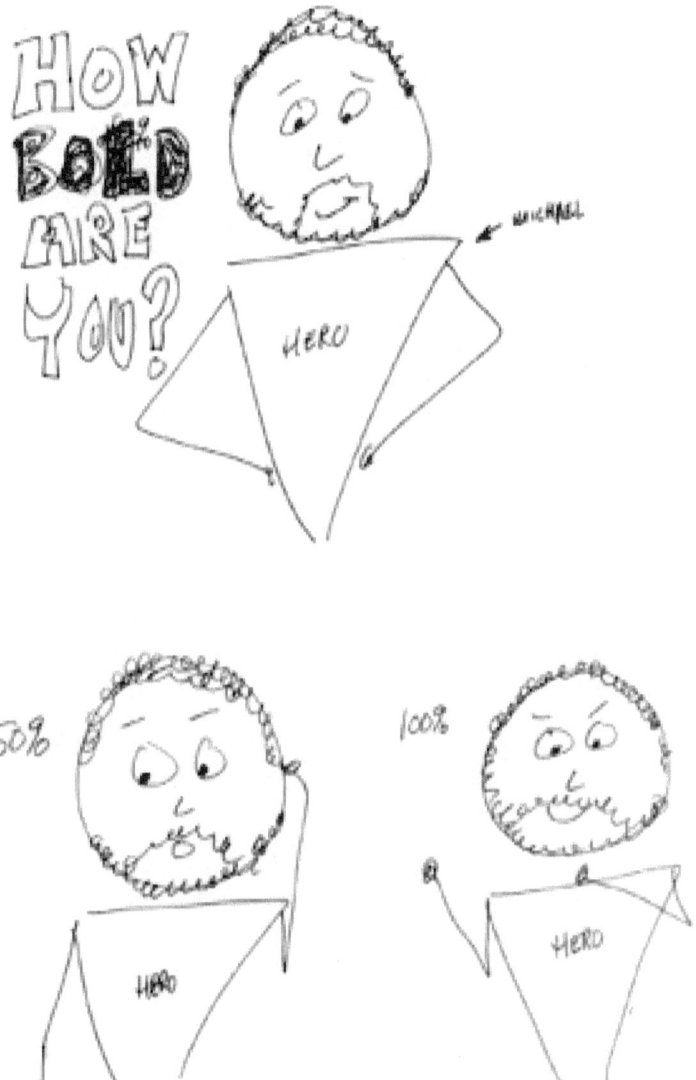

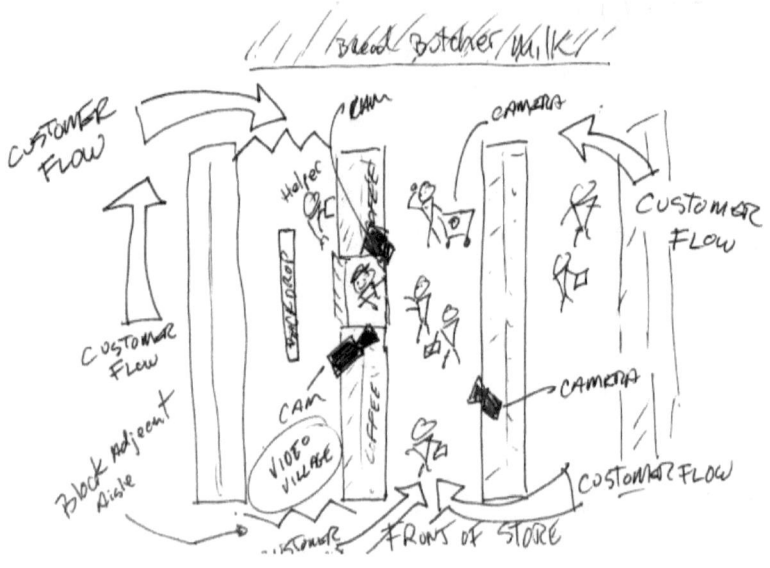

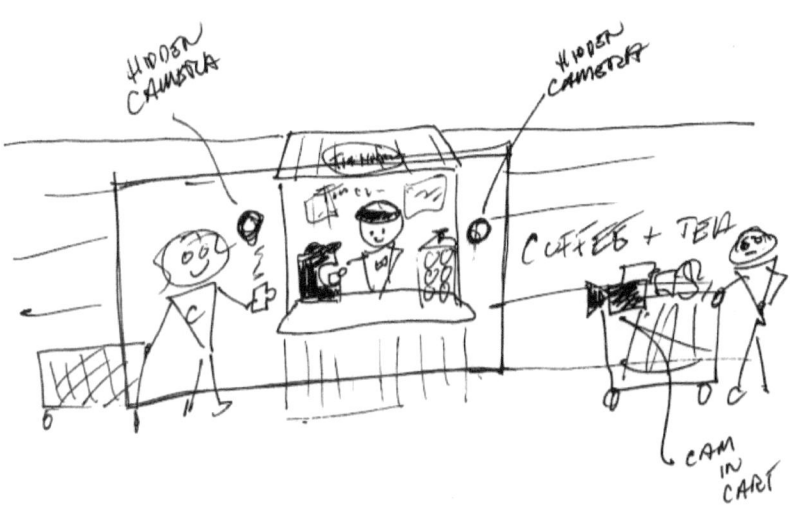

Notes.

Okay, I'm gonna be totally honest here, I needed these few extra pages to make this a better book. Under 100 pages and the binding is crap. So I did this for you. Well, us. And I do seriously want you to scribble thoughts and doodles here on these last pages. Send me your filmmaking cheats, tips and musings.

ABOUT THE AUTHOR

Jordan Brady is a multi-hyphenate and fun to Google.

He has directed four feature narrative films, the "I Am Comic" trilogy, 1,000 commercials and one comedy special.

A former nightclub comedian, Jordan is credited with coining the now ubiquitous phrase "bow chicka bow wow", for which he receives absolutely zero royalties.

He lives in Los Angeles with his wife and four kids.

HOT SAUCE

Be sure and try Oso Delicious hot sauce. A subtle blend of flavorful serrano chillis, a little garlic, a squeeze of lime and just a hint of habanero. Oso Delicous is made in the USA by wild bears. Great on eggs, tacos, pizza, eggplant, rice cakes, ribs, stew, chips and anything you can think of, except oatmeal.

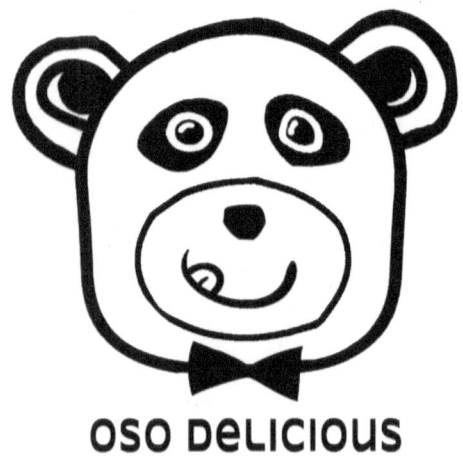

OSO DELICIOUS

www.osodelicious.org

www.ingramcontent.com/pod-product-compliance
Lightning Source LLC
Chambersburg PA
CBHW031442210526
45464CB00005B/2306